LIGONIER VALLEY

V I G N E T T E S

LIGONIER VALLEY
VIGNETTES
TALES FROM THE LAUREL HIGHLANDS

JENNIFER SOPKO

Charleston   London

THE
History
PRESS

Published by The History Press
Charleston, SC 29403
www.historypress.net

First published 2013

Manufactured in the United States

ISBN 978.1.60949.582.4

Library of Congress CIP data applied for.

CONTENTS

CONTENTS

FOREWORD

The Delaware established a village in Ligonier Valley at the crossroads of two Indian paths possibly as early as 1727. By the time of the Forbes campaign of the Seven Years' War, just over thirty years later, the Indians had abandoned Loyalhanning. The British strategy to take Fort Duquesne entailed building fortified posts across Pennsylvania, and so the Forbes Road and Fort Ligonier came into being.

Promises to the Indians notwithstanding, white settlers surged over the Alleghenies, many even before hostilities ceased. Some of those choosing to migrate to Ligonier had been here with the army; some of their descendants are here still.

It seems that once Ligonier Valley has been discovered, it lodges in your heart and soul. For those of us who grew up here, in any time period, it has been a magical place. More recent immigrants have come because of what they heard and saw.

These stories, seen through fresh eyes and told by a new voice, offer a look back to the place from where we have come. Newer stories are constantly being created and will become part of our history, to be told at a time in our future.

I have known Jennifer Sopko since May 2004 as an extraordinary researcher and a gifted writer. She has here put her talents to relating our stories in a manner that I know will be appreciated by both long-time and newer residents as well as visitors to the Ligonier Valley.

Read…and enjoy!

SHIRLEY G. McQUILLIS ISCRUPE
2012 Awardee of the Arthur St. Clair Historic Preservation Award for
Preservation of the History of Ligonier Valley
Pennsylvania Room Archivist, Ligonier Valley Library
January 2013

PREFACE

L ocated about fifty miles southeast of Pittsburgh in the picturesque Laurel
Highlands region of southwestern Pennsylvania, the historic Ligonier
Valley is forever linked to events and people that shaped American history.

Although the valley is secluded between the Laurel Mountain and
Chestnut Ridge Ranges of the western Allegheny Mountains, Ligonier was
no hidden force in the course of American history. During the French and
Indian War, Fort Ligonier served as the final supply post on the Forbes Road
and the keystone of Great Britain's successful campaign to force the French
from Fort Duquesne and take control of the "Gateway of the West" at the
site of present-day Pittsburgh.

The Ligonier Valley continues to influence the lives of both its residents
and the visitors who flock there to enjoy its scenery and history. As a pleasant
rural spot only a day's excursion from the city, this "mountain playground"
was considered a rural escape for Pittsburghers in the nineteenth century.
The scenic valley attracted attention from Judge Thomas Mellon and
other notable businessmen who supported the industrial and recreational
development of the region.

Today, Ligonier thrives as a vibrant tourist destination and all-American
town in Westmoreland County, especially during the annual Fort Ligonier
Days, a three-day celebration that draws as many as one hundred thousand
people to the town every October to recognize the valley's historic significance.

Former *Readers Digest* editor and Ligonier resident Ralph Kinney Bennett
described Ligonier as a road town in the valley's 2008 sestercentennial
publication. Indeed, one underlying theme in Ligonier's history is roads,

as several routes, from dirt trails to iron rails to asphalt, have passed through the area and played an integral part in the Ligonier Valley's development.

Before the first white man set foot in the sprawling valley, the area was marked by Indian trails along which these native people traded. In colonial days, the Forbes Road cut across the Pennsylvania wilderness west from Raystown (present-day Bedford) to the confluence of the Allegheny, Monongahela and Ohio Rivers, passing through Ligonier. In post-colonial times Ligonier became a popular destination for travelers along the Philadelphia-Pittsburgh Turnpike, the Pennsylvania Turnpike, the Lincoln Highway and U.S. Route 30.

For seventy-five years, the Ligonier Valley Rail Road not only gave outsiders access to the beautiful region, but it also transported natural resources out of the valley that were used to pave some of Pittsburgh's streets and feed the hungry steel mills that helped to build America.

Ligonier can also be described as a crossroads town, literally and figuratively, a concept which is highlighted by Bob Stutzman, co-founder of the Ligonier Valley Rail Road Association. "It's a crossroads community," said Stutzman, pointing out the symbolic intersection of roads at the middle of town, with the recognizable white bandstand at the center. Throughout the historic Ligonier Valley, visitors will discover a merging of not only roads but also of cultures and industries, as well as a sense of maintaining a balanced aesthetic between historical and modern, commercial and unique.

The road town of Ligonier can be considered a two-way street. Not only did the Ligonier Valley develop from an unsettled wilderness in pre-colonial times into a thriving industrial area and now a scenic and historic American town, but also its people continue to look back on the historical events that shaped both the region and the country's development. The 1908 "Old Home Week" sesquicentennial celebration, the 1958 bicentennial celebration (attended by President Eisenhower), the 2008 Ligonier sestercentennial celebration and all the annual Fort Ligonier Days in between show that history is valued and celebrated in the Ligonier Valley. In 1994, the Ligonier Historic District, which encompasses about 60 percent of the borough and 155 years of history, was listed on the National Register of Historic Places.

In my own experience, all of my personal roads do seem to lead to and from the Ligonier Valley. Ligonier is where my professional writing career began, at a Ligonier Borough Council meeting that I covered in October 2003 for the *Latrobe Bulletin*. Ligonier is where I have developed interpersonal

This view of the bandstand at the center of town was taken from the northwest corner of the Diamond. *Photo by Sosimo Banales.*

relationships with research contacts, mentors and friends. Somehow, I always seem to interpret a Ligonier connection in many of the stories I write.

My primary goal in this publication is to share vignettes of historical events, places and personages about which I've had the privilege to research and write. I hope this book serves as a crossroads itself, of stories not always remembered or recognized and familiar history that has endeared the valley to its local inhabitants, visitors and historians. While not a comprehensive history of the valley, I hope this book serves as an addition to the multitude of wonderful resources that have been written about Ligonier and the history contained within the valley.

ACKNOWLEDGEMENTS

M y heartfelt thanks go out to all of the wonderful people and organizations that have supported this project and my writing since I first began my career. First and foremost, thank you to The History Press for this tremendous opportunity, and, in particular, to my editor Hannah Cassilly, for your continued patience and encouragement throughout the duration of this project.

Without publications such as the *Latrobe Bulletin*, the *Ligonier Echo* and the *Westmoreland History Magazine*, I would not have a professional writing career in the first place. Thank you to Steve Kittey at the *Latrobe Bulletin*, Sue McFarland at the *Tribune-Review* and Lisa Hays and Jim Steeley at the Westmoreland County Historical Society for granting the necessary permission to reprint my work and giving me opportunities to learn more about the Ligonier Valley.

To my mentor, Shirley McQuillis Iscrupe: I cannot thank you enough for your priceless friendship, knowledge, resources and advice that have nourished me since I first began writing about this wonderful region. It is an honor and privilege to have your kind words preface my work.

Thank you to the Ligonier Valley Library, most particularly the Pennsylvania Room led by Shirley Iscrupe and Barbara Banales, for giving me complete access to your wonderful and invaluable resources.

To Brian Butko: Our paths have crossed multiple times during the course of various research projects, and I am immensely grateful for all of the advice and help you have generously given to this budding writer.

Acknowledgements

Thank you to Annie Urban, Jeff Graham and the Fort Ligonier Association for welcoming me with open arms and allowing me to immerse myself in the history contained within the fort's walls.

My thanks also go to Bob Stutzman, Bill Potthoff and the Ligonier Valley Rail Road Association for your help in my narration of what I believe to be the most fascinating stories in the Ligonier Valley's modern history.

Thank you to all of the wonderful people and organizations who have generously contributed their invaluable time, hospitality, stories, photos and proofreading for this book. In no particular order they include: The Pennsylvania Room at the Ligonier Valley Library; Annie Urban, Jeff Graham and the Fort Ligonier Association; Bob Stutzman, Bill Potthoff and the Ligonier Valley Rail Road Association; Lisa Hays and the Westmoreland County Historical Society; Matt Strauss and the Thomas & Katherine Detre Library and Archives at the Senator John Heinz History Center; Jeff Croushore and the Idlewild Park Archives; Brian Butko; Paul Fry; Cordelia Lindsay; Barbara and Sam Banales; Rose Stepnick; Harry Frye; the Latrobe Area Historical Society; Michele Sopko; and David Zajdel.

In addition, thank you to many others who I had the pleasure of connecting with over the years when conducting research for my local history newspaper and magazine stories, including Vernie West; Joe Gruebel; Harry Lattanzio; Bob Nolan; Stan Wall; Mary Lou Rosemeyer; Ralph Kinney Bennett; Janet Hudson; Drew Banas; Patti Campbell; Helen and Duane Craig; Brad Craig; Carla Baldwin; Brad Heberling; Rod Beck; Stacey Robinson; Angela Rado; Rita Horrell; Kurt Rose; Elaine Cramer Voke; Cliff Cramer; Roy Hutchinson; Richard Macdonald; James Snodgrass; Willie Ulery; Michael Kraus and the Soldiers and Sailors National Military Museum; Richard Saylor and the Pennsylvania State Archives; and many other dear people.

I must also thank my friends and family, including my parents, Carol and Michael, and my sister, Michele, for your continued love and support of all of my endeavors. Thanks to Jewels Phraner for inspiring my website, which led to my relationship with The History Press. Finally, I have to thank David Zajdel for your constant love and support throughout this project, which have given me the courage and self-confidence to continue writing. Thank you for encouraging me to follow my dreams!

THE LIGONIER VALLEY

Crossroads of American History

Loyalhanna: Indian Predecessors in the Ligonier Valley

When the Virginia-based Ohio Company sent British explorer Christopher Gist to visit and survey land west of the Allegheny Mountains in the early 1750s, he encountered various Indian tribes and settlements and reportedly visited the village of Loyalhanning, according to his travel diaries. He is considered the first white man to visit and write about what is now known as the Ligonier Valley in the mid-eighteenth century.

The name Loyalhanna is synonymous with the Ligonier Valley and has been tied to its history for over two hundred years. The primary waterway in the immediate area, the Loyalhanna Creek, runs through the Ligonier Valley. The creek's name is derived from the Indian words *loyal*, meaning "middle," and *hanna*, meaning "river." This "middle river" was situated midway between the Juniata and Ohio Rivers. Various references to this area include "Loyalhanning," "Loyal Hanon," "Loyal Hanna" and "Loyalhanna."

Indeed, there was an Indian village or campsite in the vicinity of present-day Ligonier called Loyalhanning. However, historians dispute the actual location of the Loyalhanning Indian village; it is unknown if the village was actually located where the town of Ligonier is laid out today or in the nearby vicinity instead.

As part of Westmoreland County, the historic Ligonier Valley generally stretches from the Conemaugh River south to the Fayette County boundary and from Laurel Mountain west to Chestnut Ridge, according to Shirley McQuillis Iscrupe, lifelong valley resident and Pennsylvania Room Archivist for the Ligonier Valley Library. This region, carved in the thick stone of the Allegheny Mountains, is located about an hour southeast of the city of Pittsburgh, Pennsylvania. Although the rural area and the city are separated by a distance of fifty miles, their histories are inextricably intertwined.

However, prior to Ligonier's founding as a permanent village and long before Pittsburgh became the leading producer in the steel industry, only Indians traversed the mountains, valleys and forests of this region and named the landscape using their native tongue. In the mid-eighteenth century, the southwestern Pennsylvania region was populated by various American Indian tribes including the Iroquois and Delaware.

During this period, the land was marked by various Indian trails and paths along which these tribes traded hides, furs and other goods with each other and the European explorers who inevitably discovered the area. A significant crossroads of Indian trading paths and trails existed in the Ligonier Valley. The north–south Catawba Trail and the east–west Raystown Path intersected where the town of Ligonier is located, close to where North and South Market Streets (also designated as State Route 711) and East and West Main Streets cross at the center of town, in the public square known as the Diamond.

The Post at Loyalhanna: Path to Pittsburgh

By the mid-eighteenth century, the Indians were no longer the sole actors on the North American stage. European explorers from Great Britain, France and other countries rounded out a diverse cast of characters who would act out a dramatic story.

It is conceivable that the course of American history might have taken a vastly different turn if not for a fortified military stockade built in Ligonier during the colonial period. The valley's origins trace back to the establishment of this post in the midst of a European power struggle for dominance in North America.

By the mid-eighteenth century, the French had explored southward from Canada after establishing a fur trading monopoly in North America. With a growing naval force, Great Britain was likewise exploring the new land and establishing colonies westward. In general, European explorers were navigating through North America, claiming land and establishing territories while trading with the various tribes of Indians who already lived there. The crossing of paths between the Europeans and Indians and among the European nations that were simultaneously exploring the new world during the colonial period naturally caused disputes over land ownership, especially between Great Britain and France, whose history as rivals reaches as far back as the eleventh century.

According to Jeff Graham, head of the Interpretive Programs Department at Fort Ligonier, waterways were the most expedient way to travel as well as trade and transport goods in colonial times. Territories served by significant water sources were highly desirable. The St. Lawrence River was an important fur- and skin-trading route for the French. The Mississippi River provided explorers with access to the Midwest and the rest of the unexplored new world. Connected to both of these routes, the Ohio Valley Region was a priceless area with the confluence of three waterways located at the current site of Pittsburgh, Pennsylvania: the Ohio River, the Allegheny River and the Monongahela River.

Any power that controlled the Forks of the Ohio would obviously benefit greatly from this "Gateway to the West." By 1748, there were at least six jurisdictional claims to this land: two European nations (Great Britain and France), two American colonies (Pennsylvania and Virginia) and two Indian nations (the Iroquois and the Ohio Valley Indians). Not only were European nations fighting over this land, but British colonies were also contesting each other's legal claims while the original Indian owners were struggling to defend their property.

After multiple clashes during the eighteenth century, Great Britain and France eventually came to war over this key territory in southwestern Pennsylvania. In North America, this conflict is generally known as the French and Indian War (1754–1763), but it is considered internationally as part of a larger conflict called the Seven Years' War (1756–1763), which involved battles on every continent except Australia and Antarctica.

In 1753, the Ohio Company of Virginia, a land speculation company, had begun constructing Fort Prince George at the Forks of the Ohio. However, the French moved in, expelling the British from the area, and established Fort Duquesne at the confluence of the three rivers, thereby assuming control of this important gateway from 1754–1758. Named after Michel-Ange Du Quesne de Menneville, the Governor of Canada, Fort Duquesne was the last of a line of French forts that stretched south from Lake Erie.

The British failed to regain the fort in two sequential campaigns, the first of which was led by a young Colonel George Washington in 1754. In 1755,

General Edward Braddock carved a road from Fort Cumberland (located at present-day Cumberland, Maryland) toward Fort Duquesne; but his troops were badly beaten, and the general was mortally wounded in the infamous battle along the Monongahela River.

After these two failed campaigns, William Pitt, Great Britain's new secretary of state, assigned Scottish General John Forbes to lead a westward advance across Pennsylvania in the summer of 1758, with the intent to capture Fort Duquesne. This was one portion of a major three-pronged attack against France. Forbes determined that the most strategic way for the British to usurp control of the fort was to conduct a "protected advance" of British regulars and colonial troops along a road fortified with supply posts constructed at regular intervals. Where previous British campaigns, such as Braddock's, had failed was in their lack of a defensive position to which they could retreat.

During the Forbes Expedition of 1758, the British generally followed preexisting roads west across Pennsylvania from Philadelphia through

This view shows two entrances to the reconstructed Fort Ligonier. The path in the foreground is the Forbes Road, which passed through the fort itself. The Bedford or east gate in the background is considered the main entrance. The Pitt or west gate is in the foreground. *Photo taken by Jennifer Sopko.*

Carlisle and then to Raystown (present-day Bedford), but when the troops reached Fort Bedford, they began carving a brand new road west through the virgin Pennsylvania wilderness, known as the Forbes Road. Clearing a twelve-foot-wide road across Pennsylvania was an extremely arduous task, considering troops had to cross three mountain ridges—the Alleghenies, Laurel Mountain and Chestnut Ridge—and overcome thick forests, rough terrain and swamps. To complicate matters, the British and colonial troops faced political difficulties with hostile Indians who generally allied with the French although some tribes were friendly to the British.

General Forbes's plan included the construction of a "post of passage" every fifty miles or so along the Forbes Road where troops could assemble and supplies could be sent. The final supply post built before the road reached Fort Duquesne was located on a small hill near the Loyalhanna Creek between two ridges of the Allegheny Mountains.

On September 3, 1758, work began on the Post at Loyalhanna when Colonel James Burd arrived with a contingent of troops. He supervised the

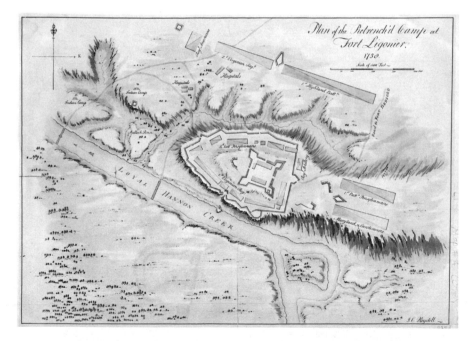

This map of Fort Ligonier was drawn by J.C. Pleydell in 1758. The "Plan of the Retrench'd Camp at Fort Ligonier" shows a strategically built form on a hill near the "Loyal Hannon Creek." *Courtesy of the Thomas & Katherine Detre Library and Archives at the Senator John Heinz History Center.*

construction of the fort at a site chosen by Sir John St. Clair. Colonel Henry Bouquet, Forbes's second in command, arrived several days later, followed by Colonel George Washington in October. Work continued on the fort's stockade and storehouses during this time and would not be completed until the spring of 1759. Engineer Harry Gordon, captain of the Royal Americans, is credited with the building of the fort.

The Post at Loyalhanna was built using the fort-construction methods of the day, which included the palisade wall on the west side—a fence comprising twelve to sixteen-foot-tall pointed wooden stakes that were tightly bound together—plus a double–horizontal log wall on the east side. The fort was also composed of angular structures known as bastions and was surrounded by a retrenchment.

According to Graham, the Post at Loyalhanna was really "a fortified base camp for military operations elsewhere." Indeed, the fort was not built to defend a strategic location but rather to serve as the final supply depot and assembly point for King George II's regular army and the colonial regiment. It was the most crucial of the four garrisons that were built along the Forbes

Lieutenant Archibald Blane of the Royal Americans sketched this representation of Fort Ligonier on June 30, 1762. The original color sketch is on display at the Fort Ligonier Museum. *Courtesy of Fort Ligonier.*

Road. Having this base of operations enabled the British to assemble troops and gather supplies before setting out in pursuit of Fort Duquesne. In this way, they were a self-supported army of multiple brigades that could come to each other's aid if needed, explained Graham.

A Strategic Crossroads at Loyalhanna: Fighting for the Forks of the Ohio

The Post at Loyalhanna can be viewed as a crossroads of history: if alternate decisions were made, and the French and Indian War ended in a French victory, this change in the dominant power in the New World could have altered the course of American history. How different would the world be today? Of course we cannot know with any certainty what would have happened under these different circumstances, but we do know the results of a decisive battle at the post and General Forbes's decision to press on toward Fort Duquesne as winter approached in 1758.

The most significant battle fought at the Post at Loyalhanna occurred on October 12, 1758, when the French retaliated after a hasty British advance upon Fort Duquesne about a month prior. This battle is referred to as both the Battle of Fort Ligonier and the Battle of Loyalhanna. On September 14, 1758, Colonel James Grant led a force intended only to reconnoiter Fort Duquesne and gather information about its defenses, but he instead decided to launch a foolish frontal assault against the French and their Indian allies.

Unfortunately, the disorganized skirmish ended in Grant's capture and defeat of the British and colonial troops, who retreated back to Loyalhanna. On October 12, the troops stationed at the garrison faced a retaliatory attack from the French. At around eleven o'clock that morning, about 1,200 French soldiers and a few hundred Indian allies fired on the Post at Loyalhanna. Led by Colonel Burd, who was in command of the fort that day in Colonel Bouquet's absence, the English contingent of 2,200 men successfully withstood the attack from the enemy, which lasted for about four hours, with little loss of life compared to the French.

After trekking along the Forbes Road across central Pennsylvania, an ailing General Forbes finally arrived at the Post at Loyalhanna in early November along with the rest of the British army. The British and colonial armies reached a strategic crossroads in late 1758 with winter approaching: should they hunker down at Loyalhanna and wait to launch a spring campaign against Fort Duquesne, or should they continue on and immediately try to drive the French from the Forks of the Ohio without any confirmed intelligence of the condition of the French army at the garrison?

At a council of war on November 11, Forbes originally decided to camp at Loyalhanna during the winter as the risks of a military advance outweighed the potential benefits. Luckily, intelligence received from prisoners captured the next day during an attack on the fort revealed that the French forces at Fort Duquesne were weak as their Indian allies had left, regular troops had moved out and supplies were low. Forbes made the crucial decision to press on west, his troops carving the last section of the road through the western Pennsylvania wilderness from Loyalhanna to Fort Duquesne.

Three divisions led by Colonel George Washington, Colonel Archibald Montgomery and Colonel Henry Bouquet left Fort Ligonier on November 15 and continued to cut a road toward Fort Duquesne. Weakened and facing an approaching British force of about 2,500 men, the French set fire to Fort Duquesne and fled, leaving the British to find the charred ruins of the fort when they arrived there on November 25, 1758.

This photo shows an aerial view of the reconstructed Fort Ligonier. Headed by renowned architect and fort historian Charles Morse Stotz, the reconstruction of the fort began in 1953 and was based on contemporary maps, written descriptions and archaeological digs. *Photo taken by Sosimo Banales.*

Claiming the site for Great Britain, General Forbes named it Pittsburgh, in honor of William Pitt. The British also rebuilt the ruined garrison and named it Fort Pitt. The capture of Fort Duquesne and subsequent establishment of Fort Pitt in November 1758 marked a turning point in the war for Great Britain and enabled the nation to build itself into a world power and an empire.

Forbes also renamed the Post at Loyalhanna, calling it Fort Ligonier after his superior officer, Lord John Ligonier, who was then commander in chief of the British army. Fort Ligonier is a significant military post for several reasons. It was never taken by an enemy during its tenure as an active military post, not during the French and Indian War or the brutal Indian attacks that plagued settlers in the 1760s. Also, its existence as a supply post and place of retreat helped the British army occupy Fort Duquesne without a battle.

George Washington:
A Secondary Cast Member on the Global Stage

Before George Washington achieved glory as the commander of the Continental army in the Revolutionary War and America's first president, he played a pivotal role in earlier events that occurred during the French and Indian War. The trials and tribulations that the young colonel experienced primed him for the colonies' later war for independence from Great Britain. He is one of the most intriguing historical figures from the French and Indian War and in the Ligonier Valley primarily because he was nearly killed right here in the area.

Washington's military career began in southwestern Pennsylvania during the 1750s as this Virginia officer fought with the British and colonists against French expansion in North America. Although Jeff Graham described George Washington as a "secondary cast member" in the drama that unfolded compared to Forbes and Bouquet, his integral roles during several acts influenced the plot of the war.

"He ultimately is responsible for starting a world war," said Graham, pointing to the twenty-two-year-old Washington's diplomatic mission to deliver a message to a French commander in 1753, demanding the country's retreat from the Ohio River Valley. Unsurprisingly, the French refused to acquiesce, and the first seeds of war were planted between Great Britain and France.

George Washington was only twenty-six years old when he led one of three divisions of British and colonial soldiers from the Post at Loyalhanna to occupy Fort Duquesne in the final leg of the 1758 Forbes Expedition. This portrait of the young colonel, painted by American artist Rembrandt Peale, is featured at the Fort Ligonier Museum. *Courtesy of Fort Ligonier.*

Afterward, the young Washington was involved in three expeditions centered on control of the Forks of the Ohio. Virginia governor Robert Dinwiddie sent him to help protect the Fort Prince George project at the confluence. En route, his troops encountered a French scouting unit, and the battle that ensued resulted in the death of French leader Joseph Coulon de Jumonville, who Washington was later accused of assassinating. Later, in

July 1754, the French got their revenge when Washington surrendered at Fort Necessity on July 4, 1754, after a failed attempt to take Fort Duquesne.

The following year, Washington accompanied General Edward Braddock as his senior American aide on the ill-fated attempt to capture Fort Duquesne and organized a retreat after the battle went south. In 1758, he also led one of the three divisions participating in the final successful advance upon Fort Duquesne in November 1758 during the Forbes Expedition.

Graham described Washington as an incredibly lucky man, who narrowly missed losing his life on the battlefield several times. After the bloody battle along the Monongahela River that cost General Braddock his life, Washington's uniform was pierced with bullet holes. However, his most infamous escape from death was during an incident that occurred only a few miles from the Post at Loyalhanna. Washington's career almost ended prematurely on the evening of November 12, 1758, when the twenty-six-year-old was nearly killed by friendly fire attempting to stop two corps of the Virginia regiment, led by himself and Lieutenant Colonel George Mercer, who mistakenly fired on each other in the dark. The two units collided near the fort while trying to surround a contingent of about 140 French soldiers and Indians who were attempting to raid the fort. At great personal risk to himself, Washington stepped in the midst of the fire of bullets, knocked his men's muskets away and called for the soldiers to cease their fire when he realized the dire situation.

Washington's only firsthand account of this incident appears in what is known as the "Remarks"—an almost eleven-page manuscript written in 1787–88 in which the fifty-five-year-old details his experiences thirty years prior during the French and Indian War, including the friendly fire incident near the fort. The "Remarks" are a series of Washington's comments and notations on a proposed biography of himself prepared by close friend and former aide-de-camp Lieutenant Colonel David Humphreys and were never meant to be published. In fact, Washington asked Humphreys to return or burn the documents after using his comments, which, thankfully the biographer failed to do.

Translated by the staff of the Papers of George Washington at the University of Virginia, Washington's comments on the friendly fire incident and the "imminent danger" he was in appear below as in the manuscript:

> *Previus* [sic] *to this, and during the time the Army lay at Loyalhaning a circumstance occurred wch* [sic] *involved the life of G.W. in as much jeopardy as it had ever been before or since*[.] *the enemy sent out a large*

detachment to reconnoitre [sic] our Camp, and to ascertain our strength; in consequence of Intelligence that they were within 2 Miles of the Camp a party commanded by Lt. Colo. Mercer of the Virga [Virginia] line (a gallant & good Officer) was sent to dislodge them between whom a Severe conflict & hot firing ensued which lasting some time & appearing to approach the Camp it was conceived that our party was yielding the ground upon which G.W. with permission of the Genl called (for dispatch) for Volunteers and immediately marched at their head to sustain, as was conjectured the retiring troops[,] led on by the firing till he came within less than half a mile, & it ceasing, he detached Scouts to investigate the cause & to communicate his approach to his friend Colo. Mercer advancing slowly in the meantime—But it being near dusk and the intelligence not having been fully dissiminated among Colo. Mercers Corps, and they taking us, for the enemy who had retreated approaching in another direction commenced a heavy fire upon the releiving [sic] party which drew fire in return in spite of all the exertions of the Officers one of whom & several privates were killed and many wounded before a stop could be put to it[,] to accomplish which G.W. never was in more imminent danger by being between two fires, knocking up with his sword the presented pieces.

Despite this near calamity within the Virginia regiment, the event was incidental to General Forbes's decision to immediately proceed with the advance to Fort Duquesne instead of waiting out the winter. During this skirmish, which left thirty-eight soldiers and two officers either missing or dead, the British took three prisoners of war, including an Englishman from Lancaster County who divulged the weak state of the French at Fort Duquesne. The British and colonial troops capitalized on this valuable information and successfully drove them from the Forks of the Ohio without a battle, finding the abandoned ruins of the burned garrison when they arrived on November 25, 1758.

George Washington's dramatic escape from harm during the November 12 incident is remarkable because his death, at only twenty-six years old, could have affected the outcome of the Forbes Expedition. Who would have led one of the three divisions that occupied Fort Duquesne in later November 1758? His death may also have had serious repercussions for the American colonists during the Revolutionary War. Who would have commanded the Continental army? Furthermore, who would have guided the new country as the first president of the United States?

History Continues at Fort Ligonier Today

After the French and Indian War, Fort Ligonier functioned both as a supply post for Fort Pitt and also protection for the villagers who settled in the Ligonier Valley. The last major battle that occurred at the fort was during Pontiac's War in 1762–63 when Indian chief Pontiac's tribes launched a war against all of the British forts, including Fort Ligonier. Still, the fort did not fall.

Fort Ligonier was decommissioned in March 1766 and placed under the responsibility of Arthur St. Clair, who served as the civilian caretaker at the fort and later became a Revolutionary War hero as major general. Years passed and most likely no above ground traces were left of the original structure by the end of the eighteenth century.

Yet the absence of a visible fort by no means diminished the Ligonier Valley's remembrance of the history that happened there. In 1927, the William Kenly Chapter of the Daughters of the American Revolution purchased the land on which the original fort stood. The organization erected a monument dedicated to Fort Ligonier in 1934, which was eventually moved to its current location on the front lawn of the current Fort Ligonier Museum.

Fortunately, the history of Fort Ligonier is preserved today through a full-scale reproduction of the original fort and an adjacent museum that were established on the original grounds. In 1953, construction began at the original location of the fort. The project was based on original plans, period maps, written descriptions and archaeological excavations conducted at the site under the direction of Charles Morse Stotz, renowned architect, historian and expert on eighteenth-century forts in North America. The excavations also yielded a collection of historically significant artifacts from the fort's active period that is preserved at the fort.

The Fort Ligonier website describes the makeup of the restored garrison:

> *Eight acres of the original site of Fort Ligonier have been preserved, with the subsurface features restored and the above-ground elements reconstructed. The inner fort is 200 feet square, defended by four bastions and accessed by three gates; inside is the officers' mess, barracks, quartermaster, guardroom, underground magazine, commissary, and officers' quarters. Immediately outside the fort is General Forbes's hut. An outer retrenchment, 1,600 feet long, surrounds the fort. Other external buildings include the Pennsylvania hospital (two wards and a surgeon's hut), a smokehouse, a saw mill, bake ovens, a log dwelling and a forge.*

In September 1958, the town held a bicentennial celebration that included a visit from President Dwight D. Eisenhower, who helps add the Fort Ligonier Bicentennial Link to the three-century chain in this photograph. *Courtesy of the Pennsylvania Room, Ligonier Valley Library.*

Today, the Fort Ligonier Association, a private nonprofit group, maintains and operates the fort and neighboring museum, which was added in 1962. According to Annie Urban, director of marketing and development at

Fort Ligonier, the historical site annually draws an estimated twenty-three thousand visitors, including student groups, families and individuals from the region, across the country and even internationally.

Visitors can also view hundreds of artifacts and thirteen original artworks in the museum. With the exception of a few reproductions, the objects on display are authentic pieces from the eighteenth century and provide visitors with a genuine experience of the time period.

Along with key players General John Forbes and Colonel Henry Bouquet, George Washington is justly represented at the museum with the rare Washington Collection that includes his original "Remarks" and a painting by American portrait painter Rembrandt Peale of the young colonel dressed in his military uniform (painted circa 1825–50). In addition, the collection features a pair of eighteen-inch-long flintlock saddle pistols—the Marquis de la Fayette's gift to Washington when the French officer joined the colonists to fight during the American Revolution in 1778. These slender, intricately decorated weapons were not worn on the body but instead were designed to fit in saddle holsters on the officer's horse.

Jeff Graham and fellow actors strategize before a battle reenactment during the town's annual Fort Ligonier Days in October 2012. *Photo taken by Jennifer Sopko.*

The museum also boasts an extensive exhibition on what Winston Churchill described as the "first world war" because of its wide-ranging scope. The exhibition is entitled "The World Ablaze: An Introduction to the Seven Years' War" and consists of two hundred original artifacts from the eighteenth century gathered from all around the world, including an authentic British regimental coat from 1760.

Since 1960, the Ligonier Valley has commemorated the October 12, 1758 Battle of Fort Ligonier with a three-day outdoor festival each October. The annual Fort Ligonier Days event attracts as many as one hundred thousand people to the town to enjoy food and craft booths, a parade, battle reenactments and artillery demonstrations at the fort and other entertainment.

Portions of this vignette appear in the original article published in the *Latrobe Bulletin*. ("Fort Ligonier Celebrates Historical Leaders During Busiest Season," April 9, 2011.)

LIGONIER

A Settled Community

Ramseytown

After the unsettled colonial period of the French and Indian War, the violent Indian attacks of the 1760s and the tumultuous Revolutionary War, settlers established permanent homes in the Ligonier Valley, which developed into a farming community and truly took shape during the early nineteenth century. Hotels, inns, taverns, stores and other amenities were established to service both the visitors who passed through the town in convoys of wagons and horse-drawn buggies as well as the settlers who stayed to raise families.

Credited as the founder of Ligonier, it was Colonel John Ramsey (sometimes spelled Ramsay), who laid out the town as it generally exists today. The Ramsey family was originally from Chambersburg, Pennsylvania, and John Ramsey eventually became a large landowner in the Ligonier Valley, thanks to land he inherited from his father, Major James Ramsey.

Spending £121, Ramsey purchased a 672-acre tract of land on September 2, 1794, when it went for bid in a sheriff's sale. Originally owned by Major General Arthur St. Clair, the land was one of three plantation tracks St. Clair conveyed to Thomas Galbraith in 1777. In addition, it was part of a tract of land referred to as St. Clair's Octagon, the only octagon-shaped tract of land ever warranted in Pennsylvania.

Using part of this land, Ramsey sketched an orthogonal grid of lots, dated March 3, 1817, which comprised what is currently the center of Ligonier

This image is of a reprint of John Ramsey's original layout for the town of Ligonier created in 1817. *Courtesy of the Pennsylvania Room, Ligonier Valley Library.*

Borough and subsequently sold these 130 individual lots to prospective homeowners. The plan also included a space for a church, an academy and a public square. Ramsey's original layout of the town hasn't changed much since 1817, despite the ebb and flow of businesses over the years and various endeavors to renovate the town and stimulate its commerce.

After initially purchasing the property, Colonel Ramsey called this village "Ramseytown," and the name stuck for years after. However, when he divided it up into sellable lots, he changed the name to "Wellington" after the duke who infamously defeated Napoleon Bonaparte at the Battle of Waterloo in 1815. Nevertheless, the name Ligonier was announced in the newspaper weeks later for the "new town laid out at Old Fort Ligonier."

Perhaps the impetus for this land development thirteen years after Ramsey purchased the land was the establishment of the Philadelphia-Pittsburgh Turnpike, which came through the area in 1817. At any rate, Ramsey seemingly had some notion of or desire for civic growth in this new village as he incorporated building deadlines and monetary penalties into the sale of lots in his development, particularly the corner lots around the Diamond along Main Street.

The most punitive condition required that buyers of the corner Diamond lots that crossed with Main Street build a "two-story house of

Looking east down East Main Street from the Diamond, circa 1948. *Courtesy of the Pennsylvania Room, Ligonier Valley Library.*

either brick (or frame painted)" within seven years or they would incur a $100 penalty, which would fund the construction of public buildings. Ramsey had hoped that the town of Ligonier would be a candidate for the county seat if a new county had been established separate from Westmoreland County.

Although Ligonier never became a county seat, the township of Ligonier was established in 1822, and the town was officially incorporated as a borough on April 10, 1834. Throughout the town's development, those corner lots around the Diamond grew with the establishment of various public buildings, from taverns and hotels to churches, stores and shops. Today, the Diamond boasts a stately Georgian-style town hall on the northeast corner, the warm and inviting Valley Library on the northwest corner, the beautiful stone Ligonier Heritage United Methodist Church on the southwest corner and multiple shops and eateries that extend in all four directions.

The Diamond: Gem of the Ligonier Valley

The open space at the center of John Ramsey's plot plan is known today as the Diamond. This beautiful public space not only functions as the heart of social and commercial activity for Ligonier but also is a source of pride for its residents. The Diamond radiates from the crossroads of North and South Market Streets and East and West Main Streets.

Historically, similar diamond plans for Pennsylvania towns usually designated this area for farmers markets and space for hitching wagons on market days, but they later were used as public park space or large intersections for vehicles. During the nineteenth century, Ligonier's Diamond served as a corral and parking area for Conestoga wagons, horses, cattle and stagecoaches until the borough council designated it as Diamond Park in 1894. The park was landscaped and fenced in to keep horse and buggy traffic controlled. The main thoroughfare was described as muddy and impassable before it was paved in 1908.

The highlight and most recognizable landmark of the Diamond is the domed covered bandstand, located on the inner diamond and surrounded by beautifully groomed landscaping, brick walkways, metal benches and wooden purple martin birdhouses. The bandstand has been a staple of the town for over a century.

A music pavilion has stood at the center of the Diamond since at least 1891, perhaps earlier. Considered one of the best bands in Westmoreland County, the Ligonier Coronet Band entertained the town with free evening

Right: This panoramic shot of the Diamond was taken during Old Home Week, Ligonier's sesquicentennial celebration, in 1908. Welcome arches were installed at all four intersections around the Diamond. *Courtesy of the Pennsylvania Room, Ligonier Valley Library.*

Opposite, top: Circa 1908, this vintage postcard depicts the bandstand surrounded by posts that were used to hitch horses. *Courtesy of Pennsylvania Room, Ligonier Valley Library.*

concerts at the pavilion and was instrumental in replacing the structure with a new one in 1894.

The new pavilion, modeled after the World's Fair music pavilion, was formally dedicated on September 27, 1894, with a grand celebration. It was designed by Pittsburgh architect Reverend S. Munsch and constructed by W. A. Menoher for a cost of $300, which was raised by subscription. The project was under the direction of a committee formed by the Ligonier Coronet

Diamond, Ligonier, Pa.

This image was taken from the inner diamond looking east down East Main Street. One of four Civil War cannons and cannonball groups placed around the bandstand is the focal point of this picture. These decorations were removed and donated for the World War II scrap metal drive. However, they were never melted down or reinstalled on the Diamond. *Courtesy of Cy Hosmer.*

Although North American purple martins no longer migrate to Ligonier each year, the multilevel birdhouses that welcomed these feathered visitors still decorate the Diamond, St. Clair Grove and various residences around town. This image is circa 1953. *Courtesy of the Pennsylvania Room, Ligonier Valley Library.*

Band. The borough renovated the bandstand in the 1920s and eventually replaced it with the current structure in 1968. Today, the bandstand continues to host free concerts throughout the year, and couples often choose the romantic spot on the inner diamond for their wedding ceremonies.

Various vintage pictures and postcards show the inner diamond accented by four Civil War cannons and accompanying cannon balls, one grouping on each side of the public park. Weighing over seven thousand pounds each, the cannons were originally donated to the Ligonier Grand Army of the Republic (a Union veterans' organization) by prominent Greensburg businessman and congressman George F. Huff around 1890. The relics decorated the Diamond until 1942 when the borough council sold them to the American Locomotive Company of Latrobe to be melted down into scrap metal for the war effort. Although the cannons and cannonballs were removed, sent to the plant and split in two, they were never melted down or reinstalled on the Diamond, according to Shirley McQuillis Iscrupe.

Although the cannons are long gone, several multilevel birdhouses that accessorize the town still remain on the inner diamond, available for feathered tenants. Colonies of purple martins, a type of North American swallow, used to visit Ligonier in the spring and summer, but a series of years with unseasonably cold weather plus effects from Hurricane Agnes in 1972 seem to have dissuaded the birds from returning to the valley and residing in manmade homes as they had done for hundreds of years.

Ligonier's Metal Sentinel: The Diamond Drinking Fountain

A small New York village is forever linked with the Ligonier Valley, thanks to a ninety-year-old piece of Ligonier history that helped the village recover a lost part of its own.

Paul Fry, Ligonier Borough's public works director, accepted an invitation to visit Babylon, New York, from the village's board of trustees in May 2011. He attended the Memorial Day unveiling of a replica of a nineteenth-century public drinking fountain, the creation of which would not have been possible without the loan of Ligonier's own historic fountain, which celebrated ninety years on the inner diamond in 2011.

Babylon's original landmark—a Victorian-style zinc drinking fountain topped by a statue of a woman feeding a dove—was erected in 1897 on a street corner in the village's town square, one similar to Ligonier's town square. The monument served as a symbol of civic pride and provided clean drinking water for people, dogs and horses in the bayside village, located on the south shore of Long Island.

The fate of Babylon's drinking fountain remains somewhat of a mystery. Christopher Proto, a local dentist, began researching the fountain's history and discovered that it was removed in the summer of 1917 amid public health concerns. One legend floating through the community is that a runaway trolley damaged the fountain and that the original pieces are rumored to lie at the bottom of a local creek.

Proto's extensive research of surviving examples of this type of fountain led him to Carol Grissom, a conservator at the Smithsonian Conservation Institution and expert in American zinc statues. Grissom informed him that Ligonier possessed a similar man-and-beast fountain that might serve as a model for a replacement of Babylon's lost one. The village planned to replace their lost piece as part of a community initiative to restore historical aspects of the village, beautify the community and generate economic development.

Except for a few repair trips back to its birthplace, Kentucky-based Stewart Iron Works Company, Ligonier's ten-foot-tall, 1,020-pound sentinel has guarded the Diamond for nearly a century. The sanitary drinking fountain is

This zinc drinking fountain has served man and beast for almost a century in Ligonier Borough although it no longer offers cool refreshing water. Before it was renovated in 2010, the fountain had a green tint. *Photo taken by Sosimo Banales.*

located on the north side of the inner diamond near the bandstand area facing North Market Street. It was a gift from the Ligonier Volunteer Hose Company No. 1, which voted to purchase it from Stewart Iron Works, then based in Cincinnati, on June 30, 1921, for $594. The company had been fundraising for a fountain since 1913.

According to Fry, a Stewart Iron Works catalog helped identify the Ligonier and Babylon fountain models as "Drinking Fountain for Man and Beast No. 209." The fountain originally provided water for people and also allowed dogs and horses to drink using two separate troughs. The fountain and its decorative moulds are actually made out of zinc, a metal resistant to corrosion by the elements, Fry explained. However, the base is composed of case iron, and the lady holding a dove that adorns the top of the piece is bronze, he added.

The Ligonier fountain's own fate was in question in February 2003 when a Pennsylvania Department of Transportation grader, traveling too fast, smashed it into several pieces. Luckily, Stewart Iron Works came to the rescue and restored the piece at a cost of $38,000.

After communications between Proto and Fry and a follow-up visit by Suffolk County legislator Wayne Horsley, in fall 2009, the borough council gave permission to ship Ligonier's ornate fountain back to Stewart Iron Works to be dismantled, cleaned and used to make castings for the Babylon replica. As compensation for the loan, the Ligonier fountain was completely restored and reinstalled on the Diamond after Memorial Day in 2010. Once green, the fountain is now a deep, glossy brown.

Thanks to a $50,000 Suffolk County grant secured by New York senator Owen Johnson, as well as fundraising efforts from a committee of residents and elected officials, the village raised over $120,000 for the new fountain. Stewart Iron Works installed the replica outside of the Village of Babylon Historical & Preservation Society Museum.

Grateful to Ligonier Borough's willingness to help them with their project, Babylon's board of trustees invited Fry to attend their 2011 Memorial Day celebration and fountain dedication ceremony, which was attended by one hundred residents and dignitaries on a hot afternoon in the village.

"You want to see the most wonderful little village that I saw in my life—I was so impressed with the generosity, the open arms and how much that that town appreciates what Ligonier Borough did for them," said Fry, who participated in the Memorial Day parade and activated Babylon's new fountain for the first time at the ceremony. He said that the plaque next to the fountain reads, "This historical reproduction would not have been possible without the help and cooperation of the people of Ligonier, Pennsylvania."

Fry spoke highly of the hospitality he received from the trustees, mayor, public works department and residents of the village—a picturesque, two-and-a-half-square-mile commuter community of only 12,615 residents, with beautiful homes, wide streets, a gazebo, four hundred lampposts decorated with hanging flower baskets and an aesthetic reminiscent of Ligonier.

Along with a favorable impression of the little Long Island village, Fry returned to Ligonier with two proclamations from Babylon's mayor, Ralph Scordino, thanking Ligonier Borough for its "civic dedication, compassion and commitment to the preservation of American heritage."

Today, Babylon celebrates a new historic era with the return of a lost landmark while Ligonier celebrates the fortitude of a landmark that has survived for almost a century. The Ligonier and Babylon fountains are truly sister fountains, sharing the same aesthetics and origins, serving as historic landmarks in their respective town squares and reaching milestones in 2011.

"We preserved our history by letting them restore their history," said Fry.

This vignette was edited from the original version published in the *Latrobe Bulletin*. ("Ligonier fountain celebrates 90 years on Diamond," June 21, 2011.)

Fostering Literary and Civic Improvement: The Ligonier Valley Library

Since 1968, the Ligonier Valley Library has stood at the northwest corner of the Diamond, beckoning patrons of all ages to come inside and get lost among the stacks.

Today, the library functions as a social center, hosting cultural and educational programs, providing specialized research materials and offering seventy thousand volumes of classic and modern literature.

While the library has adapted to cultural and technological changes during its lifetime, its goals remain rooted in a community love of reading and the civic improvement of Ligonier.

Although the Ligonier Valley Library Association celebrated its sixty-fifth anniversary in 2011 and the current building at 120 West Main Street debuted in the late 1960s, a library presence in Ligonier actually dates back to the late nineteenth century.

In December 1944, the Woman's Club of Ligonier opened the first club library at Weller's Hardware, which was located on the southeast corner of the Diamond. *Courtesy of the Pennsylvania Room, Ligonier Valley Library.*

The Ligonier Library and Reading Association filed articles of incorporation on March 21, 1884 and established the first library in two rooms over the banking house of J.H. Frank, eventually moving to a small building built on school property at "the corner of Market Street and Alley."

Headed by president Dr. J.T. Ambrose, the association's goal was "the cultivation of literary tastes and the diffusion of useful knowledge." Andrew Carnegie was a supporter of the association's work, donating $500 to the library in 1893.

The library's history becomes somewhat obscure by the turn of the century, but despite possible financial challenges and membership decline over the years, the three-thousand-volume establishment was still in existence in 1899. Evidence suggests that the library was absorbed by the Ligonier Valley School District when the Dickinson School was built on North Market Street in 1903.

The story of the Ligonier Valley Library picks up a quarter century later, when the Woman's Club of Ligonier established a public reading circle in 1930. The club was established two years prior in 1928 "to foster literary programs and to further civic improvements in the community."

Members could join the reading circle by donating a book. Thirty-five members joined at the circle's inception, with Mrs. J. Wilbert Clopp serving as chairwoman of the Woman's Club Library Committee at the time.

The first club library opened at Weller's Hardware store in December 1944, and then moved to a rented room in the Naugle Building at 135 West Main Street. This new location opened on July 14, 1945, with two hundred

On July 14, 1945, The Ligonier Valley Library reopened in a rented room in the Naugle Building at 135 West Main Street. *Courtesy of the Pennsylvania Room, Ligonier Valley Library.*

donated books on the shelves and was first operated by the Woman's Club Library Committee followed by an organized board of trustees.

Moving forward, the Ligonier Valley Library Association (LVLA) was officially incorporated on March 26, 1946, with Walter A. Saling serving as the first president. Although now a separate entity from the Woman's Club of Ligonier, the club continued to support the library, organizing fundraising events and championing for increased membership.

Under the LVLA, the library's collection grew from 2,200 volumes in 1946 to 12,852 volumes in 1949, requiring additional space for the growing collection. The LVLA purchased a two-story yellow brick residence at 223 East Main Street, which opened on August 1, 1950, with 16,000 volumes on the first floor, eventually expanding to the second floor in 1959.

During this period, teacher Vernie West and her husband, John, lived on the second floor of the building, moving in after the couple married in 1952. West, who still lives in Ligonier, said she had an early love of reading and interest in libraries, volunteering at the Ligonier Valley High School library, where she eventually taught English and Spanish.

She happened to be in the right place at the right time to fill the shoes of librarian for the downstairs library. After leaving teaching full time to raise a family, West was asked to take over as librarian in 1955 when the current librarian left, shocking the town when she married at seventy years old.

West happily accepted the paid position, which she held until March 16, 1956. She remembers that the library was a busy place and many residents used it back in those early days.

Although West resigned as librarian after the birth of her first child, she has remained active with the library, volunteering at the library's bookstore, Re-Readables, and during periodic used book sales, sorting through the donations.

"I think it's a fantastic library. We treasure it and use it constantly. I don't know what I'd do without a library," she said.

The Ligonier Valley Library made its transition from a primarily volunteer organization to a professional organization with paid staff on July 12, 1968, when the association dedicated a new modern building to house the now 25,000-volume collection at 120 West Main Street.

Designed by architect Charles M. Stotz, of the Pittsburgh firm Stotz, Hess and MacLachlin, and built by Dill Construction Company, the modern Georgian-style sandstone building replaced the former Ligonier House. The new library was made possible by a generous gift of land from original LVLA charter members Lieutenant General and Mrs. Richard K. Mellon and funding from the Richard King Mellon Foundation.

Completed in 1968, the modern Georgian-style building that currently houses the Ligonier Valley Library sits on the northwest corner of the Diamond at 120 West Main Street. *Photo taken by Jennifer Sopko.*

With a new building and increased funding and support, the Ligonier Valley Library continued to grow into the hub of activity it is today.

From its humble beginnings as a reading circle among a small group of civic-minded ladies sharing their personal volumes, the Ligonier Valley Library has become a member of a countywide network of libraries sharing multiple media among thousands of people. Those original ideas—the love of reading and community—continue today in Ligonier, only reaching more people.

However, "It's still very personal," said library director Janet Hudson.

Although the Woman's Club of Ligonier has disbanded, along with its reading circle, the library continues to promote monthly book discussion groups including "Tea and Titles" and "Death in the Stacks."

Despite the fact that the library is a full business with staff, it's still supported by a group of volunteers, who loan materials to the Pennsylvania Room for its annual photo show, sell books at Re-Readables like Vernie West and help out in the children's wing.

"That's what really sets our library apart. There's always been people who are always willing to get involved," said Hudson.

This vignette was edited from the original version published in the *Ligonier Echo*, a *Tribune-Review* publication. ("Library's history stretches back through century," July 7, 2011.)

The Ligonier Opera House

In early twentieth-century America, opera houses drew the wealthy elite and the working class together in the cultural sphere. The privileged community founded and patronized many of these stage venues, yet opera houses attracted an economically and socially diverse audience and brought both professional theater companies and local amateur actors to their stages.

According to the late Greensburg historian Robert Van Atta, early opera houses featured "traveling professional show troupes, locally produced amateur theatricals and early day burlesque." Whether because of changing tastes, financial worries or new management styles, opera houses transitioned from featuring live stage entertainment into multi-use community venues and movie houses. These establishments served as lecture halls for civic organizations, functioned as church group meeting places and hosted public high school commencements.

Among other theatrical establishments in southwestern Pennsylvania, opera houses operated during a period of prosperity in the coal and coke industries in the late nineteenth and early twentieth centuries. Cultural activities like dramatic plays and vaudeville shows presented the working class with opportunities to socialize and escape from everyday life.

The Ligonier Opera House had a more humble beginning than its southwestern Pennsylvania contemporaries, such as the Showalter Theater in Latrobe, the Monessen Opera House in Monessen and the St. Clair Theater in Greensburg. A barn built on a farm owned by Howard Cavode at the corner of Fairfield and Vincent Streets was converted into the opera house, which celebrated its grand opening on April 5, 1889. After changing ownership several times and falling into disuse, the venue was sold for timber in early 1915.

The history of the original barn's conversion into an opera house is somewhat unclear. The *Ligonier Echo* reported two conflicting accounts: first,

Ligonier Echo Wednesday, October 27, 1976

Echoes of the Past...

OPENING OF THE LIGONIER OPERA HOUSE

"It is with feelings of pleasure we are called upon to announce to the readers of the ECHO that the School Hall will be opened next Friday, April 5th, under the most favorable circumstances. A great many of our readers will recall the deplorable condition the hall has been allowed to remain in for a number of years. The present Board of enterprising School Directors have taken this matter in charge and have succeeded in making a very pretty and attractive hall. The stage has been enlarged to double its former size and the interior of the building has been artistically papered and painted. Two dressing rooms have been erected and an elegant drop curtain placed in position. A handsome painting, representing the background, graces the stage. By special arrangement Byron W. King, in charge of Curry School of Elocution and Dramatic Culture, Pittsburgh, has been secured for the opening of the Ligonier Opera House. Mr. King comes highly recommended. The program will embrace character sketches, readings, recitations, impersonations, dialect renditions, Shakespeare characters, heroic and pathetic, sentimental and humorous. It will be an evening of laughter and tears, in illustrating many various uses of voice, rare iimitations and ventriloquism. He will be assisted by his sister, Miss King. Home talent will also be present with excellent music. The proceeds are to defray the expenses of fixing up the hall. Let everybody come out and show to our School Directors that their efforts are appreciated." (Ligonier Echo, April 3, 1889)

(Photo Courtesy of Lawrence Jenkins)

N.B. The old School Hall/Opera House was located on the lot at the corner of Fairfield and Vincent Streets.

William L. Iscrupe

The Ligonier Opera House may have looked nondescript from the outside, as seen in this newspaper photo, but it was reportedly very elegant on the inside. *Courtesy of the Pennsylvania Room, Ligonier Valley Library.*

that the barn was sold to a prominent Johnstown physician who converted it, and second, that the school board renovated what may have already been used as a school hall. A picture from the *Ligonier Echo* depicts a modest wooden structure standing in a field; the interior reportedly contained an expanded stage, dressing rooms, elegant drop curtain and painted background.

The opening night program of the Ligonier Opera House is an excellent example of how the opera house mixed professional performers and local talent, combining a program from the director of Pittsburgh's Curry School of Elocution and Dramatic Culture and "home talent." Home talent also performed at the opera house in *From Sumter to Appomattox* in March 1907—a popular military war drama set in Charleston, South Carolina, during the Civil War.

This vignette was edited from the original version published in the *Westmoreland History Magazine*. ("From Stages to the Silver Screen: Early 20th Century Opera Houses Provided Diverse Entertainment for Westmoreland County," Summer 2010, Volume 15, Number 1.)

THE IRON HORSE IN THE VALLEY

Ligonier's Industrial Revolution

The Iron Horse: The Ligonier Valley Rail Road

By the early nineteenth century, when John Ramsey laid out the general plan for the town, Ligonier had grown from a supply post and stockade to a military settlement and then to a permanent village. A settled community meant the development of farming, commerce and eventually industry, which flourished thanks to a new mode of transportation introduced to the valley.

It can be argued that the modern history of the Ligonier Valley began with the establishment of the Ligonier Valley Rail Road, which connected the isolated valley with the rest of the country through a connection with the Pennsylvania Railroad located in the nearby city of Latrobe, Pennsylvania. This short-line railroad was yet another significant road in Ligonier, fit for the iron horse, which brought new people, commerce and industry in and out of the valley and sparked the region's economic growth during the mid- to late nineteenth century.

The concept of a narrow gauge railroad connecting Ligonier and Latrobe was originally conceived in 1852, but by the Panic of 1873, the line was unfinished and bankrupt after several unsuccessful ventures by local entrepreneurs. Several years later, in August 1877, former judge and prominent Pittsburgh banking magnate Thomas Mellon purchased the railroad as a business enterprise for his four sons, primarily Andrew and

Idlewild Park, near Latrobe, Pa.

A Ligonier Valley Rail Road engine chugs through the Loyalhanna Gorge near Idlewild Park in 1910. Today, the westbound lanes of U.S. Route 30 pass through this area. *Courtesy of the Pennsylvania Room, Ligonier Valley Library.*

Richard, who transformed it into a commercial success, proving to their father that purchasing the defunct railroad was a worthwhile investment.

Finally, after twenty-five years in the making, the first run of the Ligonier Valley Rail Road left Latrobe bound for Ligonier on December 1, 1877. From Latrobe, the nearly eleven-mile main line passed southeast through Derry Township along the banks of the Loyalhanna Creek through Ligonier Township, arriving in the town of Ligonier. To save expenses, the Mellons initially decided on a narrow gauge operation (a smaller distance between rails, at three feet) instead of a standard gauge operation, but ended up converting the line to a standard gauge in 1882.

During its entire seventy-five years in operation, the Ligonier Valley Rail Road offered consistent passenger service, transporting nine million passengers along the line, which stretched for 10.6 miles from Latrobe to Ligonier. In all, the railroad supported eleven passenger stops along the main line during its operation—nine stations and two platforms. Running west to east, these stops were located at Latrobe, Oakville, Osborne, Kingston, Bakers (platform), Long Bridge, Darlington, Idlewild, Millbank, Bells (platform) and Ligonier. In 1899, the railroad added a summer stop near Frank's Hotel, which was a popular tourist lodging in town.

Eight engines can be seen in this photograph, taken at the Ligonier Valley Rail Road wye in Ligonier, possibly circa 1890s or the turn of the century. *Courtesy of the Pennsylvania Room, Ligonier Valley Library.*

Thanks to the railroad, Ligonier residents could travel to Latrobe and even Pittsburgh faster and more easily than they did before the railroad was established. In addition, the Ligonier Valley Rail Road's passenger operations brought weekend and summer visitors from Pittsburgh who were anxious to escape city life and enjoy the natural rural beauty, not to mention the picnic grounds and amusements at nearby Idlewild Park, which was a scenic picnic area the Mellon family established to boost passenger service on the line. The concept of Idlewild Park was based on the late nineteenth-century "trolley-park" fad, which involved the construction of amusement parks along streetcar and trolley lines.

The park attracted many picnickers from the region and eventually grew into a respected and historic amusement park, as discussed in detail in a later vignette. Lines were added to the schedule to handle the increased passenger traffic to the park. In later years, the railroad added several second-hand, gasoline-powered, rail motorcars known as "doodlebugs" to the line for its passenger service as they were more economical to operate.

However, the railroad's primary revenue came from the freight service, which hauled thirty-two million tons of natural materials in and out of the Ligonier Valley, including coal from numerous mines, coke from the beehive ovens, stone from several local quarries, timber from Laurel Mountain and various manufactured goods from businesses that sprung up along the line.

On July 5, 1912, a Ligonier Valley Rail Road passenger train and a freight train collided with each other at a blind curve by the harness racing track at Denny's Flats near Wilpen. The accident caused the deaths of twenty-three people. *Courtesy of the Pennsylvania Room, Ligonier Valley Library.*

Beginning around 1900, the Mill Creek Branch, sometimes referred to as the Wilpen Branch or the Ligonier-Wilpen-Fort Palmer Branch, was added to the line in stages after the organization purchased the unfinished Westmoreland Central Railroad. The 5.4-mile extension of the line accessed the numerous coal mines and coke ovens northeast of Ligonier at Wilpen and Fort Palmer. The coal mines harvested the famous "Pittsburgh Coal Seam" in the region.

For all of its prosperity, the Ligonier Valley Rail Road's history has not been without its share of tragedy. On July 5, 1912, the railroad's two channels of revenue came to a deadly crossroads. A passenger train and a freight train collided on the Mill Creek Branch of the line when both rounded a blind curve near the harness racing track at what was known as Denny's Flats near Wilpen.

The horrific accident resulted in the deaths of twenty-three passengers and crewmen and many others injured. A fully loaded passenger coach was being pushed north from Ligonier while another engine pulling a forty-car coal train was heading south back to Ligonier. Although the passenger train's conductor, Charles Kuhn, saw the oncoming freight train and tried to reverse the direction of the passenger train, it was too late to avoid a collision.

The accident was caused by a miscommunication in the verbal orders given to both conductors involved in the accident. Harry Knox, the freight train's conductor, received verbal permission from the dispatcher to override the schedule of the passenger train and leave Wilpen as he was behind schedule. Kuhn was notified to hold his train until the freight train left but somehow misconstrued the order and thought that the train was already in Ligonier when he started conveying his passengers north to Wilpen. The railroad was held liable for the accident and suffered financial and legal repercussions for years after this incident.

In the twentieth century, the Ligonier Valley Rail Road's business improved during World War I and World War II, thanks to the demand for coal and other materials for the war efforts. However, by midcentury, after many prosperous years hauling freight and transporting passengers in and out of the region, the Ligonier Valley Rail Road entered into a decline.

The Ligonier Valley Rail Road transported thirty-two million tons of freight and nine million passengers in and out of the valley over seventy-five years in operation. The railroad folded after a period of decline in the mid-twentieth century, with its final run occurring on August 31, 1952. This picture was taken from the train at the Ligonier station facing west. *Courtesy of the Pennsylvania Room, Ligonier Valley Library.*

The Great Depression, the growing popularity of the automobile and other available forms of freight transportation were all factors that doomed the line. The Ligonier Valley Rail Road ceased operations after its final run on August 31, 1952.

Over time, traces of the Ligonier Valley Rail Road have slowly faded from Ligonier, although some vestiges remain as testaments to the railroad's influence in the development of the valley. Where iron rails once cut through the Loyalhanna Gorge, the westbound lanes of U.S. Route 30 now transport motorists on the former rail bed. A portion of the rail bed in Ligonier Township has been repurposed into a hiking and biking trail as part of the recreational board's Rails to Trails initiative. Most of the stations and platforms have been demolished. Over the years several organizations have occupied the Ligonier station.

In 2004, railroad enthusiasts Bob Stutzman and Bill McCullough established the Ligonier Valley Rail Road Association in order to preserve the legacy of the Ligonier Valley Rail Road, conserve its vestiges, collect relics and memorabilia and educate the public about railroading in the valley. Today, the non-profit association manages the Ligonier Valley Rail Road Museum, located in the beautifully restored Darlington Station near Idlewild Park.

Feeding the Steel Mills and Paving the Streets of Pittsburgh: Industry in the Ligonier Valley

Today, Ligonier is not characterized as an "industrial" town, but in earlier days, its economic development was due to several industries in the valley that profited from the rich abundance of natural resources found in the mountains, including stone, timber and, most notably, coal. The joining thread between these industries was the Ligonier Valley Rail Road, which enabled these materials to be transported out of the valley for use elsewhere.

In his 1918 history of Westmoreland County, *Old and New Westmoreland*, John N. Boucher described the Ligonier Valley as chock full of natural resources during the valley's industrial revolution:

> *That part of the township which lies close to and includes part of the ridge or mountain, is hilly and is of little value for agricultural purposes. For the last forty years it has yielded a great deal of lumber. Great quantities of*

stone have also been quarried from the mountain side [sic]. *The interior of the valley is richer in agricultural wealth, and its diversified surface is well adapted to grazing and to the production of all kinds of grain and vegetables. There are also many streams, which in the southern part flow into the Loyalhanna, the largest and most noted stream in the valley, and in the northern part flow into the Conemaugh river. The northern part of the valley is underlaid with the Pittsburgh seam of coal, having a thickness of from seven to nine feet, while the upper and lower Freeport seams are said to underlie most of the valley.*

The two most significant industries supported by the railroad were coal mining and the production of coke. Although the total number of active coal mines in the valley is unknown, at one time the Ligonier Valley Rail Road may have supported as many as twenty-two, as surmised by Bob Stutzman, Ligonier Valley Rail Road Association co-founder, interpreting a United States Geological Survey map that indicated the existence of that number of mines.

These mines harvested part of what was known as the Pittsburgh Coal Seam, which was "once recognized as being the most valuable coal bed in the bituminous coal fields of Pennsylvania," according to the Penn State Fayette

The image shows the tipple at the Old Colony coal mine around the turn of the century. The Ligonier Valley Rail Road transported tons of coal mined from the plentiful coal fields north of Ligonier. *Courtesy of the Pennsylvania Room, Ligonier Valley Library.*

Coal and Coke Heritage Center, a leading repository for the history of the southwestern Pennsylvania coal and coke industry. The center is headquartered at Penn State University's Fayette campus in Connellsville, Pennsylvania, in the midst of a region that was once an incredibly active coal bed.

Coal was an invaluable resource during the nineteenth century as it was used for domestic and industrial heating, steam production, illuminating gas production and the production of coke—a crucial ingredient in making steel as it burned hotter than coal. Although coal mines were established along the main line of the railroad in the valley's Long Bridge/Darlington and Oakville/Osborne communities, most of the coal was harvested along the Mill Creek Branch, which the Ligonier Valley Rail Road extended in order to reach those fertile coal fields north of Ligonier. The company added four stations along the almost six-mile line: North Ligonier, Hanna's Run, Wilpen and Fort Palmer.

An almost forty-mile-long portion of the Pittsburgh Coal Seam, known as the "Connellsville Coking Coal Fields" was located along the base of Laurel Mountain and Chestnut Ridge and was renowned for harvesting an extremely pure and high-quality grade of coal. This bituminous seam of coal, estimated to contain more than ten billion tons of the natural material, set a worldwide standard for metallurgical coal due to its superior composition, consistent thickness and uniform quality.

Most significantly, this coal was used to produce what is referred to as "Connellsville Coke," which was an almost 100 percent pure carbon coke used in the Pittsburgh steel mills. In short, this high quality coal produced the coke that produced the steel manufactured in America for roughly one hundred years throughout the nineteenth and twentieth centuries, and it was produced here in southwestern Pennsylvania.

According to Stutzman, there were six coking operations, or batteries of ovens, in the Ligonier Valley although the total number of individual ovens is unknown. The majority of the coking operations were also located along the Mill Creek Branch, but there was one along the main line. The Elizabeth plant, located just south of Osborne, had one hundred coke ovens in addition to a coal mine.

Another valuable resource in the Ligonier Valley was stone quarried, even before the advent of the railroad, from the mountain ridges that cradled the valley and used for a variety of construction projects. What was particularly unique about some of this stone was its dark blue tint, which inspired the commercial term "bluestone" for this particular variety of building stone. It is also referred to as Loyalhanna Limestone.

Numerous coke ovens dotted the landscape in Wilpen, a coal-mining town established about 1906–7, about three miles north of Ligonier. These ovens produced the high quality material so essential in creating steel. This image is circa 1940. *Courtesy of the Pennsylvania Room, Ligonier Valley Library.*

The bluestone harvested from some of the quarries along the Loyalhanna Gorge in the Darlington area was carved into Belgian paving blocks that were used to pave streets of major cities; it was reported that millions of tons of this material were used as paving blocks in the city of Pittsburgh alone in the early 1920s. Many road contractors chose to use the Ligonier bluestone instead of gravel as it was described as a hard surface stone able to weather a variety of conditions. Quarrymen faced a difficult task in shaping symmetrical blocks from the rough and irregular limestone that was blasted from these mountains. Understandably, the Ligonier Valley Rail Road was immensely important in transporting these heavy Belgian blocks of bluestone out of the valley.

The Ligonier Valley Rail Road supported two major bluestone quarries established on the main line along the Loyalhanna Gorge in the late nineteenth century. Located on the south side of the gorge near the Long Bridge Station, the Booth and Flinn quarry began operating in either 1882 or 1883. Research suggests that this quarry was originally developed by Hutchinson and Harrison but afterward managed by Booth and Flinn, Ltd.

Established in the late nineteenth century, the Booth and Flynn stone quarry was located along the Ligonier Valley Rail Road line, on the south side of the Loyalhanna Gorge. Stone was one of the native materials in the Ligonier Valley to be transported out of the valley by the Ligonier Valley Rail Road. *Courtesy of the Pennsylvania Room, Ligonier Valley Library.*

Later renamed the Booth and Flinn Company, the Pittsburgh-based contracting company was a partnership between James J. Booth and Pittsburgh politician and public works contractor William Flinn, who merged their ventures sometime in the last quarter of the nineteenth century (sources give varying dates as to the formation of this company, including 1877, 1881 and 1893). Headquartered in Pittsburgh, the company was considered one of the largest American general contracting companies of its time.

Booth and Flinn was responsible for most large construction and paving contracts in Pittsburgh and western Pennsylvania, such as streets, trolley lines, bridges and several tunnels—including the Liberty Tunnel (1924) and Armstrong Tunnel (1927) in Allegheny County. Perhaps it was Senator Flinn's clout as a major political boss and business magnate in Pittsburgh that earned the company those lucrative contracts.

The image shows various Ligonier Stone Block Quarry employees at work. The quarry was located on the north side of the Loyalhanna Creek. *Courtesy of the Westmoreland County Historical Society.*

The Ligonier Stone Block Company established operations on the north side of the Loyalhanna Creek at McCance (Darlington) in 1884. Over 447,000 tons of bluestone that came from this quarry was used for the Conemaugh River Lake flood control project completed in July 1952. This project, the last supplied by the Ligonier Valley Rail Road before it was disbanded, involved the construction of a dam on the Conemaugh River between Blairsville and Saltsburg, Pennsylvania. One of the tipples from the company's operations still remains along the westbound lane of U.S. Route 30.

Research also suggests that both of these quarries were actually owned by the Booth and Flinn Company at one time. Later, the Latrobe Construction Company took over ownership. One prominent local example of the projects built with the valley's native bluestone is the Heritage United Methodist Church, built in 1903 on the southwest corner of the Diamond with bluestone from a Byers-Allen Lumber Company quarry.

The Ligonier Valley Rail Road also transported timber and lumber, chiefly because of its connection with the Pittsburgh, Westmoreland and Somerset Railroad at Ligonier. Incorporated on April 15, 1899, the PW&S was another short-line railroad that ran from Ligonier to Somerset, Pennsylvania, until

The Byers-Allen Lumber Company used the PW&S Railroad to transport timber from the surrounding mountains to the company sawmill located at the eastern edge of Ligonier along the Loyalhanna Creek. *Courtesy of the Pennsylvania Room, Ligonier Valley Library.*

September 23, 1916. The PW&S was built as a means for the Byers-Allen Lumber Company to transport logs harvested from Laurel Mountain to the Byers-Allen Saw Mill located just southeast of Ligonier Borough along the Loyalhanna Creek, but it also transported passengers, coal and bluestone.

The company specialized in lumber, railroad ties, picket fences and lath, which were thin, narrow pieces of wood used to support plaster in home construction. When the lumber supply diminished, the sawmill closed in 1908 and was dismantled and sold in 1910. The railroad's demise was not far behind.

Another lumber company that serviced the region, the Ligonier Lumber Company, operated a sawmill, located about two miles north of Ligonier along the banks of Mill Creek near Oak Grove, and used the railroad to transport its lumber. The company was organized on September 20, 1913, and the sawmill closed in 1917.

The industries that flourished along the Ligonier Valley Rail Road were not limited to coal, coke, stone, timber and lumber, although those are considered the best known. The railroad also transported other natural resources and manufactured goods for businesses that developed along the line, including bark, gas, steel, paper, oil, brick, ice and even milk and mail,

This aerial view west of Ligonier near Kingston Bridge shows the Lincoln Highway, on the right, and the Ligonier Valley Rail Road, on the left, straddling the Loyalhanna Creek. The railroad tracks became the westbound lanes of U.S. Route 30 and the two-way Lincoln Highway was converted into the eastbound lanes. Also pictured are the Johnston House (now the headquarters for the Lincoln Highway Heritage Corridor), Peters Paper Mill (now a Kennametal plant) and Soisson Brick Yard. *Courtesy of Paul Fry.*

according to current Ligonier Valley Rail Road Association president Bill Potthoff. Some of the companies that benefited from the proximity of the railroad included the Pennsylvania Car Works, Consolidated Ice Company, Peter's Paper Mill, Latrobe Steel, Latrobe Construction, Vulcan Mold and Iron Company, Soisson Brick Yard, Crescent Pipe Line Pumping Station, Atlantic Refining and Kennametal's Kingston plant.

The Ligonier Station

While the western station at Latrobe was a crucial junction for the Ligonier Valley Rail Road, as it connected the line with the Pennsylvania Railroad, the eastern terminus at Ligonier was also an important crossroad for the business. First, it was the final destination for the many visitors who came to enjoy the beauty of the Ligonier Valley. Second, it served as an intersection with the Mill Creek Branch of the railroad.

Completed in 1910, the Ligonier Valley Rail Road station sits along West Main Street in Ligonier Borough. This entrance was actually the rear entrance; the tracks ran along the opposite side of the building. *Photo by Jennifer Sopko.*

Finally, it linked the railroad to the short-lived Pittsburgh, Westmoreland and Somerset Railroad.

After more than a century, the Ligonier station remains one of the stateliest buildings in Ligonier Borough. The original terminus at Ligonier was a very simple wooden building and platform that the Mellons decided to replace with a more impressive passenger station in 1909. The building and platform were moved to the opposite side of the tracks and converted into a freight station to make room for a new two-story structure measuring one hundred feet long and seventy-five feet wide. The new terminus officially opened on Saturday, August 13, 1910.

Prior to the station's grand opening, the *Ligonier Echo* touted the new station as "one of the most complete and convenient stations possible to construct, modern in every particular" and deemed it a fireproof building because of its makeup of granite, cement and tiling. According to Bob Stutzman, the Ligonier station might be constructed of a combination of solid granite in the lower level and granite-glazed terra cotta blocks above—a common ceramic architecture technique in the early twentieth century.

However, the building wasn't just modern, practical and convenient. The Mellon family wanted to attract more passenger business to the railroad as well as impress their visitors with a grand and modern building while entertaining them in Ligonier. Spending between $50,000 and $80,000 to build the structure, the Mellons created "one of the most beautiful and complete railroad stations to be found in western Pennsylvania." Described as grand, magnificent and imposing, the exterior featured a block-design façade, arched windows, a fenced roof and lion head gargoyles roaring at passengers from above the front and rear entrances.

The interior of the station was just as grand as the exterior. The main floor featured a ticket office, baggage room, general waiting room and separate men's and ladies' waiting rooms. Inbound and outbound passengers were whisked across a "very fine and pretty tile floor, with painting and frescoing that harmonize." The modern Ligonier terminus was also equipped with a steam heating system installed below the main floor, as well as plumbing and electric. Upstairs, the second floor contained fully furnished offices for management that were accented by natural-finish hardwood floors

According to Stutzman, the front entrance of the station was actually the entrance facing the railroad tracks and was recessed to give passengers a more impressive welcome when they arrived in Ligonier. Outside the station, passengers waited underneath a series of overhead sheds to board their trains.

After the Ligonier Valley Rail Road disbanded in 1952, the Southwest Division of the Pennsylvania Game Commission purchased the Ligonier Station in 1957 and used it as its headquarters. In 2002, the commission sold the building to the Ligonier Valley School District, which converted it to an administration building.

The former Ligonier station has weathered over one hundred years on West Main Street mostly unchanged, except for a few cosmetic alterations, including the gradual graying of the blocks, the addition and removal of striped window awnings and a shroud of ivy that blanketed the building at one point in time. Nevertheless, after more than a half century since the railroad came through the valley and twice that time since it first opened, the former railroad terminus at Ligonier remains "a station of which people of Ligonier valley and the owners of the railroad should be proud."

MILITARY HEROES OF THE LIGONIER VALLEY

T he strategic minds, military prowess and even human frailties of British and colonial figures like General John Forbes and Colonel George Washington helped shape the Ligonier Valley and guided America's course during colonial times. In modern times of war, the fealty and character of the people who settled in the region are embodied by the military veterans who called the Ligonier Valley their home.

The valley, deeply rooted in military history, is decorated with many monuments and tributes to the local men and women who have served in the armed forces, representing Great Britain and the American colonies in the early days and the United States after the country was founded.

For example, St. Clair Grove honors Revolutionary War Major General Arthur St. Clair, the American Legion Byers-Tosh Post 267 is named after the first two soldiers from the Ligonier Valley to lose their lives in World War I and Ligonier Valley High School—the Alvin P. Carey Memorial Building, to be exact—is named after a Congressional Medal of Honor recipient who gave his life in World War II. The Ligonier Valley can boast of many other native sons and daughters who have served America in times of war and peace since its early days.

St. Clair Grove:
A Common Area Named after an Uncommon Man

In 2001, a collaborative effort between the Loyalhanna Watershed Association, Ligonier Borough and a committee of volunteers revitalized the site of a former town dump, gas station and trailer park into a commons area for the Ligonier Valley.

St. Clair Grove, which marked its tenth anniversary on June 23, 2011, is located at the original eastern entrance to Ligonier Borough. Designed by landscape architect Shep Butler, the tree-lined grove, with its winding pedestrian walkway, metal benches and flower garden terrace, sits at the fork where East Main Street and the Old Lincoln Highway split.

Reflecting on the project a decade after its grand opening, former watershed executive director Drew Banas said he still felt a sense of accomplishment for several reasons.

"It was a good project. We improved the eastern gateway to the town of Ligonier," he said. "It was community involvement. It's something that's tangible and recognizable and has really made a difference."

The St. Clair Grove welcome terrace is located at a spur where the old Lincoln Highway (left) and East Main Street (right) split. The park's "toe" features a flower garden, a plaque honoring Major General Arthur St. Clair and a stone monument affixed with a map showing all the memorial sponsorships scattered throughout the grove. *Picture taken by Sosimo Banales.*

Banas recalled the fundraising campaign to make St. Clair Grove possible. Along with support from the Richard King Mellon Foundation, the R.K. Mellon Family Foundation and Barry and Ann Sullivan, the group secured funding through individual donations and memorial sponsorships, he said.

Patti Campbell, borough planning commission member and owner of the Campbell House Bed and Breakfast, volunteered to coordinate the collection of sponsorships for the trees, benches and lampposts at the grove. Campbell raised $200 to 400 for each tree and $1,000 for each bench.

"It was a wonderful experience for me," she said, remembering the generous response she received from the community and the people she met through working on the project. "When I drive by there I take great pride in it, I really do."

The grove features ten different species of trees planted as gifts and in honor or in memory of individuals. Ten benches designed by Butler-based Keystone Ridge Designs and six lampposts are also interspersed throughout the grove.

A focal point at the grove, located at the welcome terrace at the fork, is a large stone monument affixed with a plaque mapping all of the memorial sponsorships. Donated by the Department of Conservation and Natural Resources, the stone was found in Forbes State Forest at the former site of a Pittsburgh, Westmoreland and Somerset Railroad rock quarry, according to Banas.

He also said many familiar names in the Ligonier Valley appear on the plaque, including Bea and Harry Kline, owners of the former Kline's apparel store; Wayne "Red" Morrow, former borough public works director; as well as Banas's father, Andrew Banas, for whom he sponsored an American Holly tree.

General Richard K. Mellon and the Ligonier Valley community as a whole are among those honored in the grove.

The grove was truly "an effort of the Ligonier Valley community," as the plaque reads.

Along with fundraising campaigns, a group of volunteers also helped to line the park after it was seeded and planted annuals at the welcome terrace, which was built by Doug Bates Masonry.

Banas credited Don Carey, local professional horticulturalist, for spearheading the creation of the flower garden at the "toe" of the welcome terrace. Carey maintained the garden until this year, when Weeders and Seeders Garden Club member Dr. Wilma Light took on the responsibility.

"There was a lot of interest from community members and non-community members to help with the grove," said Banas.

Like other amenities in Ligonier, St. Clair Grove pays tribute to the valley's history in several ways.

The grove is located along the historic Lincoln Highway and also incorporates the last surviving stone entrance pillar to the borough. In the early twentieth century, two sets of pillars were erected at the east and west ends of town.

The grove is named after perhaps the most historic figure associated with Ligonier—Major General Arthur St. Clair. A second plaque highlighting his ties to the Ligonier Valley was also installed on the stone monument at the welcome terrace.

Among his various accomplishments, St. Clair served as an agent for William Penn and a caretaker of Fort Ligonier. He also fought as major general for the Continental army during the Revolutionary War, served as president of the Congress of the Confederation and was the first governor of the Northwest Territory.

Once the largest landowner in western Pennsylvania, St. Clair settled in the Ligonier Valley and spent the last years of his life on Chestnut Ridge, before sadly dying bankrupt, losing his holdings in a sheriff's sale.

Years after the park opened, Banas constantly sees people using the walking trail.

"This turned into a really nice grove. It's used quite a bit by residents," he said.

This vignette was edited from the original version published in the *Ligonier Echo*, a *Tribune-Review* publication. ("St. Clair Grove Marks 10 Years," June 30, 2011.)

A Serious Game of Capture the Flag: Private John C. Ewing

Among the over one thousand Civil War soldiers documented at the Ligonier Valley Library, one local soldier's heroic deed earned him the highest military decoration a soldier can receive.

Private John C. Ewing, one of only two Congressional Medal of Honor recipients from the Ligonier Valley, was honored for his capture of a Confederate flag during an assault on Confederate troops on April 2, 1865.

The current whereabouts of Ewing's medal are unknown, but his exploits were discovered by two of his descendants in Ligonier.

While conducting research, Pennsylvania Room archivist Shirley McQuillis Iscrupe came across Ewing's name as a Medal of Honor recipient from the area.

Iscrupe received some genealogy of the James Scott family from a cousin, which indicated that she was a descendent of Ewing—a first cousin of her great-grandfather, George W. Scott, another Civil War veteran.

"It's the way genealogy often comes together. It's called serendipity," Iscrupe explained.

She remembered the name while preparing for the library's historic photo show commemorating the 150th anniversary of the Civil War in 2011.

Private John C. Ewing was awarded the Congressional Medal of Honor for capturing a Confederate flag in a battle near Petersburg, Virginia on April 2, 1865. During the Civil War, this heroic act would cause confusion among the enemy troops as well as wound their pride. *Courtesy of the Pennsylvania Room, Ligonier Valley Library.*

Ewing was featured in the collection of Civil War veterans' photos and artifacts. Iscrupe said the 2011 event was the biggest one since the show started in 2002. It has grown to include documents and artifacts in addition to photographs loaned by the community.

"It just gets bigger every year," said Iscrupe. "The community never ceases to amaze me with their generosity."

Helen Weller Craig discovered her great-uncle's decoration in 2000, when a family member saw a solicitation from Soldiers and Sailors for information on the soldier and recognized the family name. Craig and her father, Stuart Weller, shared the middle name Ewing.

Craig's family is steeped in military experience, with family serving in the U.S. Army, Navy and Air Force in several conflicts. Her late brother-in-law, Kenneth Craig, was the only soldier born in Ligonier to reach the rank of brigadier general.

"You can be really proud that your family does all this," said Craig.

Ewing was born on March 4, 1843, on a farm in Donegal Township. On September 12, 1864, the dark-haired, hazel-eyed farmer was mustered into the 211th Pennsylvania Volunteer Infantry for a one-year term, at only twenty-one years old.

The morning after a Union victory at the Battle of Five Forks in Virginia on April 1, 1865, General Ulysses S. Grant ordered an assault against Confederate fortifications around Petersburg, Virginia.

According to Deeds of Valor, the April 2 assault on Petersburg "was of the most determined character and the losses, even to the Union forces, correspondingly severe"—a repeat of the previous day's battle. The Battle of Five Forks and the Petersburg assault led to Confederate General Robert E. Lee's surrender at the Appomattox Courthouse in Virginia.

The 211th Pennsylvania Infantry, stationed south of Petersburg, attacked a section of the Confederate line defended by the Sixty-first Alabama Infantry just after 4:30 a.m. Ewing captured a standard of the Sixty-first Alabama, one of three Confederate flags taken in the attack on a battlefield known as Pamplin Park. He was cited for his actions that day and issued the Medal of Honor on May 20, 1865.

The exact circumstances of Ewing's capture of the Confederate flag may be contained in some lost correspondence or buried with Ewing and his regiment brothers, but what is certain is that capturing an enemy flag was a significant and symbolic act during the Civil War.

Flags not only identified the center of a line on the battlefield, but they represented regimental pride. Regimental colors, considered serious pieces of equipment, were guarded by devoted color-bearers. The loss of a flag not only caused confusion on the field but also demoralized the troops.

"Most soldiers considered the potential capture of their regimental flag by the enemy as something that would bring shame and dishonor on every member of a regiment," explained Richard Saylor, archivist and military historian for the Pennsylvania State Archives.

He said that a fight for a flag could escalate into a grisly and personal affair, costing many soldiers' lives.

"It's very possible that [Ewing] was engaged in a hand-to-hand struggle with a color bearer," said Michael Kraus, curator for Pittsburgh's Soldiers and Sailors Memorial Hall and Military Museum.

"It's not just a game. These guys held onto them with their lives. They were the center of every regiment, north or south," he added.

Ewing's citation is no less remarkable for the fact that while many Medal of Honor medals are given posthumously or after many years, the surviving veteran received his little more than a month after his "distinguished gallantry in action."

After the Civil War ended, Ewing was mustered out of the army on June 2, 1865. He returned to civilian life, marrying Mary Jane Hoover and working as a traveling salesman for the W. T. Allen Company of Philadelphia for forty years. He died on May 23, 1918, in Johnstown and is buried in the Ligonier Valley Cemetery.

In October 2000, Ewing was inducted into the Hall of Valor at the Soldiers and Sailors Memorial Hall and Military Museum. He is the second of only two Westmoreland County soldiers inducted into the hall.

The library documented over one thousand Civil War veterans from the Ligonier Valley, thanks to the efforts of the staff and volunteers. Iscrupe said more research was conducted for the Civil War show than in previous years, consulting sources from the Pennsylvania Room collection, checking online databases and photographing graves at local cemeteries.

However, Iscrupe said they are not stopping at one thousand soldiers. The Pennsylvania Room collection is an ongoing research project. She encourages people to continue submitting materials as research tools for the library.

For now, what is known about Private John C. Ewing's history is preserved in the Ligonier Valley Library and with his descendants. Future information discovered on his life may shed more light on his military exploits during that hard day on a Virginia battlefield, but his Medal of Honor attests to the importance of his capture of that Alabama flag in a war that significantly altered the course of American history.

This article was edited from the original version published in the *Ligonier Echo*, a *Tribune-Review* publication. ("Medal of Honor recipient remembered for Civil War heroism," July 14, 2011.)

Lost in the Great War:
Privates William Tosh and Benjamin Byers

The Ligonier Valley gave birth to local heroes who participated in military conflicts throughout America's history, not just during the colonial period. The American Legion Byers-Tosh Post 267 is named after two Ligonier soldiers who lost their lives in World War I: Private William Tosh and Private First Class Benjamin Byers.

What is noteworthy about these two young men is that they were the first two soldiers from the Ligonier Valley who were killed during "The Great War." When Ligonier's American Legion post was established in February 1927, these two fallen heroes' names were selected to be added to the post's designation in memorial of their services on a French battlefield during the conflict.

John William Tosh was born on April 17, 1900, to John and Mary "Millie" Tosh, of Ligonier Township. He enlisted in the Pennsylvania National Guard with Company M of the 110th Pennsylvania Infantry Regiment, Twenty-eighth Infantry Division on June 15, 1917. The seventeen-year-old Tosh trained with the Twenty-eighth Infantry Division at Camp Hancock in Georgia and was eventually transferred to the headquarters signal service before the regiment deployed to Europe the following year.

About a month later, on July 13, 1917, Benjamin Franklin Byers also joined

Portrait of Private William Tosh, one of the first two men from the Ligonier Valley killed in World War I. This picture, proudly displayed at the American Legion Byers-Tosh Post 267, may be the only known existing picture of Tosh. *Photo taken by Jennifer Sopko, with permission from the American Legion Byers-Tosh Post 267.*

Company M. Described as a tall man with light blue eyes and black hair, Byers was born on July 25, 1889, to Mr. and Mrs. Daniel Byers, also of Ligonier Township. Prior to his service in the Pennsylvania National Guard, Byers was employed at the Crescent Pipe Line Company, a precursor to the Mellon family's oil industry endeavors and subsequent founding of the Gulf Oil Company. Founded by William Larimer Mellon Sr., grandson of Judge Thomas Mellon, the Crescent Pipe Line Company was an oil company that transported oil from Allegheny County to Cumberland County, with a pumping station established at the eastern end of Idlewild Park in Ligonier at what was considered the Millbank area.

Privates Byers and Tosh both served in the 110th Pennsylvania Infantry Regiment, which was a component unit of the Twenty-eighth Infantry Division of the United States Army National Guard, also known as the Keystone Division. The 110th Infantry Regiment was activated in September 1917 and its troops were sent for training at Camp Hancock and then deployed to Europe in the spring of 1918. After arriving in England, the

Portrait of Private First Class Benjamin Franklin Byers, one of the first two men from the Ligonier Valley killed in World War I. This picture is also displayed at the American Legion Byers-Tosh Post 267. *Photo taken by Jennifer Sopko, with permission from the American Legion Byers-Tosh Post 267.*

110th reached France on May 17 and 18, 1918, and encamped in an area south of the Marne River and east of Paris. The regiment was stationed near the Western Front between the Allies and Germans and fought in the Second Battle of the Marne, which was the last major German offensive in World War I and took place between July and August 1918.

The 110th Infantry Regiment was deployed to Courmont, a small French village just south of the l'Ourcq River on July 27, 1918. Two days later, on July 29, the headquarters for the 110th Infantry likewise moved to Courmont after the German army attacked its previous location in Fresnes with shellfire a day earlier. The new headquarters was located near Grimpettes Woods at the top of what was referred to as Hill 230 in the proximity of a German army stationed nearby.

On July 20, 1918, the Allies moved closer to victory, but neither Private First Class Byers nor Private Tosh would survive that day to see the outcome of the war. Both Ligonier Township natives were killed in action when the 110th Infantry Regiment led a final attack—its sixth—against the German forces at Sergy Hill. Byers was fighting on the front at Sergy Hill and died on the battlefield, succumbing to wounds received by machine-gun fire. He had only turned twenty-nine years old.

Meanwhile, the German army blew up the Courmont headquarters of the 110th Regiment, with the young Tosh working inside as a telephone operator. The heavy shellfire demolished the building and killed seventeen men. The body of eighteen-year old Tosh was found in the wreckage.

Although the July 30 battle resulted in heavy casualties for the 110th Infantry Regiment, including the loss of Private First Class Benjamin Byers and Private William Tosh, it also ended in a victory for the Allies. Tosh was originally buried in France, but his body was later sent home to Ligonier and reburied in the Ligonier Valley Cemetery on July 24, 1921. Byers remains in France, buried at the Oise-Aisne American Cemetery in Fere-en-Tardenois.

Today, the American Legion Byers-Tosh Post 267 supports its regular members of all military branches, Sons of the American Legion and Ladies Auxiliary with services and activities, yet remains cognizant of preserving the history and memories of past heroes such as Privates Byers and Tosh, whose names will be forever linked to the post.

The Ultimate Sacrifice: Staff Sergeant Alvin P. Carey

Staff Sergeant Alvin P. Carey is one of the most decorated veterans from the Ligonier Valley, receiving seven medals for his service during World War II. However, his heroic actions against the German army on a French battlefield earned him the military's highest decoration: the Congressional Medal of Honor. He is one of only two Ligonier Valley men to receive this award and of those two, the one who sacrificed his life in order to serve his country.

Carey was born on August 16, 1916, in Lycippus, Pennsylvania, but moved to Laughlintown when he was a child and grew up there with his sister Pearl. He graduated from Ligonier Valley High School in 1935 and married Anna Mae Ankney of Waterford, Pennsylvania, on October 5, 1942. The couple had no children.

What we can determine about his character through high school yearbooks and personal recollections suggest a well-rounded individual but nothing overtly predictive of the heroics he would later display on the battlefield. He was described as reserved, fond of reading and having a favorite activity of "solituding." However, the five-foot-six, muscular boy was also a team player and gifted athlete who earned his letter in football as halfback on the high school team, played baseball and was even recommended for the track team.

The twenty-five-year-old Carey enlisted in the U.S. Army on January 24, 1941, joining Company K of the Thirty-eighth Infantry Regiment of the Second Infantry Division, eventually reaching the rank of staff sergeant. Only three and a half years later, on August 23, 1944, he found himself leading a machine gun section against a strong German resistance commanding a pillbox at the crest of what was called Hill 154 near the village of Plougastel in the French province of Brittany.

After the Allied forces returned the fire raining down on them from the pillbox, Staff Sergeant Carey left his troops behind and began crawling the two hundred yards up Hill 154 toward the pillbox, armed with several hand grenades and his carbine. He shot and killed a German infantryman blocking his way up the hill and continued on toward his destination.

Once within range of the pillbox, in the midst of heavy machine gun fire, Carey began strategically throwing grenades until he landed one inside an opening, effectively destroying the pillbox and killing the German soldiers inside. Destroying a concrete pillbox took extraordinary effort and created a hole in the Germans' defenses that could be exploited by the Allied forces, according to Michael Kraus, curator for Soldiers and Sailors National Military Museum in Pittsburgh.

"Pillboxes were pretty serious obstacles and strategically placed, so to take one out took considerable courage and effort…Carey's tactic of blowing one with a hand grenade exploited the weakness of the position because a grenade explosion was contained in the box, killing all inside. The difficulty, of course, is a soldier had to get very close to lob a grenade into one of the slit windows, an act of utmost courage," said Kraus.

Tragically, Carey was mortally shot and died on the battlefield after blowing up the pillbox that day. The young man was only twenty-eight years old. However, the rest of his troops followed his lead, occupied the pillbox and overcame the rest of the German resistance in the area. Carey's family and friends back home in Laughlintown were not aware of what happened on that French battlefield until October. Before then, he had been considered missing in action.

Staff Sergeant Carey was posthumously awarded the Congressional Medal of Honor by President Truman on May 11, 1945, "for conspicuous gallantry and intrepidity at the risk of his life, above and beyond the call of duty." He was first buried in a French military cemetery, but his body was disinterred, sent home and reburied in the Ligonier Valley Cemetery on July 15, 1948.

In addition to the Medal of Honor, Carey also received the Purple Heart, Bronze Star, American Defense Medal, American Campaign Medal, European African Middle Eastern Campaign Medal and the World War II Medal during his career. After his death, Carey's heroics were memorized with multiple dedications. When the Ligonier Valley School District's new high school opened in 1964, it was named the Alvin P. Carey Memorial Building in honor of the fallen hero. According to a newspaper story recounting Carey's return home to his final resting place, an athletic field at Camp Swift in Texas, a former combat infantry training area for World War II, was named Carey Field and the American Legion's baseball diamond in Ligonier was dedicated in his honor.

Carey was also inducted into the Hall of Valor at the Soldiers and Sailors National Military Museum on March 6, 2005. He shares this distinction with fellow Medal of Honor recipient Private John C. Ewing, also from the Ligonier Valley, who received his award for capturing a Confederate flag during the Civil War.

On Veterans Day 1998, Carey's widow and his sister donated his medals to the Ligonier Valley High School. His family also donated the flag that draped his casket, which is displayed in the high school's lobby alongside his medals.

Carey's decorations were refurbished and rededicated at the Air Force Junior ROTC annual Veterans Day ceremony on November 10, 2011, at the Ligonier Valley High School. Each year, the Air Force JROTC cadet corps hosts a Veterans Day ceremony at the high school honoring all those who have served or are currently serving in the military—men and women who have made the JROTC program possible in the first place. The annual ceremony highlights the extraordinary actions of local veterans who risked their lives for their country.

Joined by two of the staff sergeant's second cousins, Elaine Cramer Voke and Cliff Cramer, the cadets displayed the shining medals to Carey's fellow veterans and families that were in the audience that night.

"We are so blessed to have him in our family…We're pretty proud of him," said Voke. Her grandfather, Albert E. Cramer, and Carey's mother, Olive Cramer Carey Allen, were siblings.

Thanks to the efforts of the JROTC, the stories of lost heroes like Alvin Carey will be preserved for succeeding generations of cadets.

This vignette was edited from original versions of articles published in the *Latrobe Bulletin*. ("LVHS Junior ROTC honors Staff Sgt. Alvin Carey, local veterans" and "Valley World War II veteran gave ultimate sacrifice to country," November 17, 2011.)

Lest We Forget: The Darlington District Honor Roll

Every year, America loses members of the generation that fought in World War II. Until the people of Darlington, a small community in Ligonier Township, stepped in, the valley was in danger of losing a monument honoring those veterans from Darlington who fought in this conflict.

Sixty-eight years after it was erected in Ligonier Township, the Darlington District Honor Roll moved under the protection of other local heroes at the Darlington Volunteer Fire Company.

Dedicated to all Darlington World War II veterans on September 5, 1943, the original honor roll stood quietly tucked along Darlington Road "at the

Charlotte Rose (now Mrs. Glenn Welshons) stands by the original Darlington District Honor Roll. Like many Darlington residents, Rose has multiple relatives listed on the plaque, including three uncles and several cousins. *Courtesy of Rita Horrell.*

intersection of the roads leading to the bridge which enters Idlewild Park," as described by a *Latrobe Bulletin* article a few days before the ceremony.

Rita Johnson Horrell and her husband, Jack, were the monument's caretakers ever since they purchased the land on which the original honor roll was built about forty years ago to construct their home. The monument weathered the passage of time, western Pennsylvania seasonal changes and two severe floods under the Horrells' care, but several years ago it was discovered to have fallen into disrepair with water damage, loose stones and a cracked foundation. As the monument was too damaged for on-site repair, the decision was made to rebuild the honor roll at a more accessible location above the township's flood plain.

According to Horrell, her father, Adolf Johnson, built the original stone structure on his property located at the end of Darlington Bridge along Darlington Road. Joseph Eaton Sr., a local woodwork enthusiast, carved the original fifty-seven names of Darlington veterans on a walnut panel that was encased in glass on the front of the monument. In 1945, after the war ended, thirty-four additional names were inscribed, bringing the total number of World War II veterans from the Darlington area to ninety-one, which includes eighty-seven men and four women.

About forty years later, in 1986, the wooden face of the monument, which had warped and faded over time, was replaced by an eight-hundred-pound bronze plaque, funded by donations from the community, the veterans' families and a sizeable contribution from Horrell's cousin, Sidney Warren Riggs.

According to the 1943 *Bulletin* article, the Senior Women's Club of Darlington fostered the erection of the honor roll and the fundraising that paid for it. In 2009, Horrell began spearheading similar fundraising efforts to move the honor roll to its new home about a mile away at the Darlington Volunteer Fire Company. She was able to solicit enough funds within a month to cover all of the expenses for the materials needed to rebuild the monument.

From fundraising to construction, the honor roll project was a cooperative effort between the Darlington community and the fire department. Firefighters Kurt and Kevin Rose, who operate Darlington Construction, volunteered their time to build the new monument, which took about a year and a half to complete. The brothers laid the foundation, built the brick casing and filled the structure with concrete. The bronze plaque was moved and attached to the new base. They also added a sidewalk and curb for easier access.

"We wanted to make something that would last," explained Kurt Rose.

According to Rose, the project was completed with help from the entire thirty-five-member fire department, including Chris Ivory, Tim Kruel, Dave Shirey, Bob Painter, Bob McDowell, John Ramsey and Bob Ramsey. An added benefit of moving the honor roll to the fire company is that the department will provide continual maintenance

"It will have perpetual care," said Horrell.

The original honor roll was celebrated with a large ceremony at the Darlington Bridge in 1943. A rededication ceremony for the new monument was held on July 21, 2012, at the Darlington fire station and included speeches from Horrell, the project chairperson; Pennsylvania State Representative Mike Reese; and Nelson Lowes, commander of the Ligonier Veterans of Foreign Wars Post 734. Entertainment featured patriotic selections by the barbershop quartet Almost Perfect and a Ligonier VFW color guard presentation.

At the time of the ceremony, only seven of the ninety-one veterans immortalized on the bronze plaque were still living, according to Horrell: John Gross, Ruth Bates Hammond, Arthur Johnson, Richard Macdonald, Wilbert Rose, James Snodgrass and James Zollinger. Five of the seven survivors attended the rededication ceremony, including Snodgrass, who served as a B-24 crewman and aviation ordnanceman in the navy, and Macdonald, a First Lieutenant in the Eighth Air Force, which was responsible for strategic bombing of enemy targets in Europe during World War II. Macdonald's family is intimately connected with the Darlington area as former owners of Idlewild Park.

Macdonald said he was proud to serve his country and have his name on the monument. "I was no different from any other veteran. We all felt very pleased to have served," he said.

Many of the names on the honor roll are familiar surnames in the Ligonier Valley, including Nicely, Riggs and Byers. "It's a small community. Pretty much everybody that's from here…at least recognizes a name on there," explained Rose, whose grandfather Wilbert Rose and great-uncles Albert Rose and Lawrence Rose are listed on the honor roll.

Likewise, Horrell's connection to the honor rolls goes deeper than her father's work on the original monument and her caretaking—she has a brother, brother-in-law and ten first cousins listed on the plaque.

Horrell came away from the honor roll construction project with an impression of how intensely the war impacted the close-knit community of Darlington and how many families were affected. In fact, many families had multiple members sent off to war.

"It seems that every able-bodied young man from the Darlington area served in World War II...I just didn't realize every household up and down this road, their sons were out there. This was our whole town. That's just what impresses me, how many of them went," mused Horrell.

This vignette was edited from the original version published in the *Latrobe Bulletin*. ("New Darlington Honor Roll honors Valley WWII vets," July 14–15, 2012.)

A Man of Passion: Brigadier General Kenneth R. Craig

Historically, the Ligonier Valley has seen significant events in American warfare and welcomed such leaders as Colonel George Washington and Major General Arthur St. Clair. However, Ligonier is also home to a distinguished commander of its own: Brigadier General Kenneth Robert Craig.

Craig is the only solider to enlist at the Pennsylvania Army National Guard Armory in Ligonier that was commissioned a brigadier general. He received the honorary rank when chosen as the deputy adjutant general for the Pennsylvania National Guard at the culmination of his forty-year career.

Craig's family remembers the distinguished public career and private life of the brigadier general, loving husband and devoted father of four. They attribute his success to a combination of character traits: common sense, practicality, a strong moral center and, above all, passion for all areas of his life—family, career and avocations.

"He was a man of passion, but it was remarkable how much he wasn't governed by it," said his son, Brad Craig.

A man committed to doing his job well, Craig inspired his officers through his leadership. In a letter from Major Bill Colvin, an officer who served under Craig, Colvin thanked his commander for the profound effect his examples of leadership and terrain tactics had on his life and career.

In addition, Craig also taught his children life lessons through his examples.

"He was the type of person that led by example, in everything that he did," said Brad Craig.

Craig followed the precept that loyalty was a two-way street.

While officers expect obedience from their subordinates, "people in charge need to give that same loyalty to those who are working under them," said daughter Lisa Hays, who kept that message in mind throughout her own career as executive director for the Westmoreland County Historical Society.

Kenneth R. Craig is the only Ligonier-born veteran to attain the honorary rank of brigadier general. *Courtesy of Lisa C. Hays.*

Born July 25, 1927, "Bob" Craig grew up in Ligonier Township through the Depression and World War II. With his younger brother Duane "Skeeter" Craig, he enlisted in the Pennsylvania Army National Guard with the Second Battalion, 110th Infantry Regiment, Twenty-eighth Infantry Division at the Ligonier Armory on March 17, 1947.

With the Headquarters and Headquarters Company, Bob and Skeeter began basic training on Monday nights in Ligonier followed by a summer encampment at Fort Indiantown Gap, a National Guard training site outside of Harrisburg, Pennsylvania.

At the onset of the Korean War, the Twenty-eighth Infantry Division was activated in September 1950 and sent to Camp Atterbury near Edinburgh, Indiana, where they trained draftees.

While Skeeter was involved in engineering, Bob worked in intelligence during his early career with the army. In early 1951, Bob studied intelligence analysis at Fort Riley, Kansas, according to his army discharge papers.

"At one point he came home and said 'I know things so secret I'm not allowed to think about them,'" recalled Hays.

When the Twenty-eighth Division was deployed to Europe to reinforce NATO, the brothers parted ways in their military careers. Skeeter left the army while Bob served with the occupation forces in Germany until July 1952.

After returning from Germany, Craig was honorably discharged from the army as master sergeant, receiving an army occupation medal for his services. He reenlisted in the Pennsylvania Army National Guard and began to ascend the military hierarchy, accumulating responsibilities and commanding larger units.

In 1954, Craig received a direct commission as a second lieutenant, transferring from infantry to armor. Promoted to captain, then major, he served as a battalion executive officer of the Second Battalion, 103rd Armor until 1968, when he transferred to the First Battalion, 110th Division, later becoming lieutenant colonel and battalion commander in 1972.

After being promoted to colonel, Craig commanded the Second Brigade, Twenty-eighth Infantry Division at their headquarters in Washington, Pennsylvania, from 1978 until his retirement. Craig analyzed and organized various military units, training them for combat-ready status.

He retired as a colonel in August 1983, but was commissioned a brigadier general when Governor Robert Casey reinstated him as deputy adjutant general of the Pennsylvania National Guard, a post he served from May 1987 until March 1989, prior to his death on June 8, 1989.

Despite his ranks and decorations, Craig shied away from recognition, preferring to let his work speak for himself, according to daughter Carla Baldwin. Although he did not have the college education necessary for promotions, he was able to reach the heights that he did on the sheer strength of his job performance.

Craig's military accomplishments serve as an example of a passionate man committed to his family, his regiments and his country—a Ligonier native whose memory lives on in the community.

"I always felt that he was officer material from the very beginning," said Skeeter Craig, describing his brother as a no-nonsense type of solider well respected by his subordinates. "It was Bob's character and hard work, not any political advantage or special privilege, that enabled him to ascend the ranks."

This vignette was edited from the original version published in the *Ligonier Echo*, a *Tribune-Review* publication. ("Family remembers general as a man of passion," May 26, 2011.)

Craig's character, strength and mental fortitude were tested in various ways as he continued his military career, eventually earning him his final appointment as deputy adjutant general. Chosen by the late Major General Gerald Sajer to serve as his second in command, Craig functioned as a liaison among the adjutant general, commanding officers and support staff and was responsible for enforcing policy and preparing regiments for emergency action.

Although Craig did not experience wartime combat, he witnessed urban combat when the National Guard was called to break up civil rights riots in Pittsburgh's Hill District following the assassination of Martin Luther King Jr. in 1968, remembered Hays. This first-hand experience may have prepared Craig for his assignment to create an urban warfare training facility. In 1988, he planned and designed Military Operations in Urban Terrain (MOUT), located at Fort Indiantown Gap.

Named "Craigtown" as a tribute to the brigadier general's accomplishments, MOUT was a "realistic training environment" used to train soldiers in urban hand-to-hand combat—forward thinking at the time. At its inception, Craigtown was one of only three such facilities in existence nationwide.

"In a way it was a forerunner of what was coming next, this urban warfare, and how to train soldiers to fight in those kinds of conditions," explained Hays.

She also remembered one critical job Craig handled while the Twenty-eighth Infantry Division trained at Fort Indiantown Gap in 1980. Craig had to arrange food and temporary lodging for tens of thousands of Cuban refugees sent to the Fort for processing after a mass exodus during an economic crisis in Cuba. He received the Humanitarian Service Medal for his service during this incident.

Craig's numerous awards and decorations also include a Legion of Merit, given to him in 1983 for his command of the Twenty-eighth Infantry Division, commending his "exceptional leadership and inordinate professionalism, innovative and imaginative programs coupled with dynamic organization ability." In addition, he also received a Pennsylvania Distinguished Service Medal for his service as the deputy adjutant general, commending his work at Craigtown.

Although this native Ligonier Township man's name isn't memorialized on any building, park or monument in the Ligonier Valley, Craig's military accomplishments and personal character are things that the Ligonier Valley can be proud of in one of its own.

Section V

ROADS AND RECREATION

Pennsylvania's Mountain Playground

Ligonier: "Pennsylvania's Mountain Playground"

The Ligonier Valley is a crossroads where industry and recreation merged in the nineteenth century to boost the development of the region. As a counterpoint to the industries that extracted the natural resources of the valley from the surrounding mountains, the rustic attractiveness of the area was also considered a natural resource in and of itself.

Ligonier's appeal as a recreational destination primarily grew around the turn of the century, thanks to the introduction of the railroad during the latter part of the nineteenth century, which brought weekenders and summer vacationers to the country from Pittsburgh. During the early twentieth century, when the country's love affair with the automobile began, entrepreneurs focused on promoting travel. Ligonier became a tourist destination along a series of significant routes that passed through the town, with roadside attractions, lodgings, taverns and roadhouses cropping up along the way, designed to make the traveler more comfortable during his journey.

As such, "Pennsylvania's mountain playground," is an apt moniker for the Ligonier Valley because it grew to offer residents and visitors enjoyable recreational activities and amenities.

A Scenic Spot on Western Pennsylvania Roadways

The town of Ligonier became a travelers' stop along the various state and national roadways that cut through the valley. Prior to the automobile age, these were dirt roads and wagon trails that carried people and products between towns. When the portion of the Philadelphia-Pittsburgh Turnpike (a string of ten turnpikes between the two cities) known as the Greensburg-Stoystown Turnpike came through Ligonier in 1817, the artery offered new opportunities for the valley from the stagecoach traffic.

Stagecoach inns such as the Ligonier House (built possibly as early as 1820), hotels like the Breniser Hotel (built in 1900) and taverns flourished in town and permanent residences increased thanks to John Ramsey's new platting of the town. Retail and commercial ventures that popped up along these routes benefited from the new residents and wayfarers that came through the region.

The introduction of the automobile in the early twentieth century allowed motorists more freedom to travel than ever before. With such opportunity, entrepreneurs not only built various roadside attractions designed to satisfy a traveler's appetite for rest, nourishment and sight-seeing, but they also formed booster organizations to promote routes and improve them with signs and pavement.

The best-known and romanticized route may be the Lincoln Highway, considered America's first named, coast-to-coast highway. Carl Fisher, an animated promoter who had just made a fortune selling his gas-powered headlight company, proposed the idea of a "coast-to-coast rock highway" in September 1912 to likeminded automobile manufacturers. A year later, in 1913, they had established the Lincoln Highway Association.

Soon after, construction began on the Abraham Lincoln Memorial Highway, which was not only America's first transcontinental highway but also the country's first national memorial to President Abraham Lincoln. The plan was to choose a route by connecting existing paths, then raise funds and buy materials that states and counties could use to build the highway. The original route stretched 3,389 miles from Times Square in New York City to San Francisco, California. The road generally followed old turnpikes and somewhat followed the Forbes Road through Pennsylvania, at least in spirit.

As named roads like the Lincoln Highway and William Penn Highway proliferated, the tangle of long names became confusing, leading the federal government to establish a highway numbering system in the 1920s.

THROUGH A GROUP OF INDUSTRIAL SUBURBS INTO PITTSBURGH
No. 1 reading from West to East, or No. 16 reading from East to West

ACROSS THE TWO MOST WESTERLY MOUNTAIN RANGES ON THIS TRIP
No. 3 reading from West to East, or No. 14 reading from East to West

This map depicts the route of the Lincoln Highway as it passes through the Ligonier Valley. "Pennsylvania's mountain playground" sits between Laurel Mountain and Chestnut Ridge in western Pennsylvania. *Courtesy of the Pennsylvania Room, Ligonier Valley Library.*

Today, much of U.S. Route 30 follows the old path of the Lincoln Highway. Portions of the original highway have been redirected, renamed and plowed under but can still be traced across the country thanks to dedicated public historians and roadside America enthusiasts such as Brian Butko, leading Lincoln Highway historian and author as well as editor at Pittsburgh's Senator John Heinz History Center.

According to Butko, the Lincoln Highway served as the main road between and through small towns. Property along this highway was prime real estate for business owners who wanted to attract the many potential customers traveling along that route. Ligonier benefited by having this national route run directly through the center of town along East and West Main Streets for about a mile. The *Ligonier Echo* described this stretch of road, which was finally paved in 1919, as "one of the finest mile drives on the Lincoln Highway between Pittsburg and Philadelphia." The Lincoln Highway utilized part of the Philadelphia-Pittsburgh Turnpike and generally followed the path of the Forbes Road with a few exceptions where the roads diverge.

"The Lincoln Highway brought almost every cross-country traveler and trucker through Ligonier and western Pennsylvania from 1913 until the bypasses began being built, up to the ultimate bypass, the Pennsylvania Turnpike," said Butko.

When congestion on the Lincoln Highway became too much, towns built bypasses, which alleviated the traffic problems but sadly hurt the businesses established in the towns. In 1928, after most of the Lincoln

Highway was renamed U.S. Route 30, a bypass was built around Ligonier and East and West Main Streets connected with U.S. Route 30 on both ends.

Butko described the network of highways west of town along Loyalhanna Creek:

> *The western end of West Main Street rejoins U.S. Route 30, but the original Lincoln Highway continued uphill, wound behind Shirey's cabins and motel and behind the Colonial Inn, then behind the antique mall. Today, that road curves back to U.S. Route 30, but the original can be seen as a trail up the next hill. It came back down the other side, crossed the stream, then ran behind the new Roadside Giant pump. It ran between Donato's Sunoco and the former Ridgeway Inn, both demolished in recent years. This was bypassed in 1928 by a road that now serves as westbound U.S. 30; a portion of this road, running through Loyalhanna Gorge, was built atop the railroad grade after 1952. Where the road splits west of the Road Toad and Longbridge, the eastbound lanes of U.S. Route 30 are the original two-way Lincoln Highway.*

This view of West Main Street, circa 1963, shows pillars from the Ligonier House on the right, a hotel demolished to make way for the current library. The concrete marker on the corner indicates that this is an original portion of the Lincoln Highway. *Courtesy of the Pennsylvania Room, Ligonier Valley Library.*

This postcard depicts the Lincoln Highway and the Loyalhanna Creek between Ligonier and Latrobe, Pennsylvania. Before the westbound lane of U.S. Route 30 was built on the north side of the Loyalhanna, the Lincoln Highway was a two-lane road here. *Courtesy of Brian Butko.*

The Lincoln Highway was originally marked by red, white and blue porcelain signs painted with the letter "L," and then cement posts with bronze medallions and the tri-color emblem were installed along the route on September 1, 1928. Today, these concrete route markers are few and hard to find. Various pictures show that there was one at each Main Street intersection on the Diamond. Although it's unknown if this is original to the location, one surviving concrete marker sits outside Ligonier's Town Hall along East Main Street.

The original Lincoln Highway has changed over the century with portions being renamed, redirected and decommissioned and quaint roadside attractions being replaced by strip malls and convenience stores. However, the history of the road is being preserved by various organizations established along the route, including the Lincoln Highway Heritage Corridor in Pennsylvania. Its headquarters are located on the cusp of the Ligonier Valley, in the former Johnston House near the Kingston Dam on the eastbound lanes of U.S. Route 30.

The Lincoln Highway Heritage Corridor is a non-profit organization that advocates the conservation and promotion of the historic Lincoln Highway, specifically focusing on the two-hundred-mile corridor of the route that passes through six Pennsylvania counties, from Adams through

Westmoreland, the latter of which encompasses Ligonier. The organization is one of twelve designated heritage areas under the Commonwealth of Pennsylvania's "Heritage PA" program.

Roadhouse Renaissance: The Washington Furnace Inn

One Ligonier Valley roadside attraction along the Lincoln Highway was the popular Washington Furnace Inn. After sadly sitting dormant and in disrepair along westbound U.S. Route 30 in Laughlintown for several years, the Washington Furnace Inn is happily entertaining patrons again after the historic roadhouse reopened in 2012 with a full restaurant, lounge and expansive bar. Not only is Washington Furnace Inn's reopening another commercial stimulant for the Ligonier Valley, but it is also a revitalization of a Lincoln Highway landmark and a remnant of days gone by when travelers needed a place to stop and refresh following a long day's drive.

After more than twenty years in the auto parts business running Heberling and Beck Auto & Truck in Latrobe, Pennsylvania, co-owners Brad Heberling and Rod Beck purchased the defunct roadhouse in November 2010. Along with Stacey Robinson, the pair worked to completely renovate the building and fulfill their longtime dream of opening their own restaurant

"It's something that we've always wanted to do. It's exciting," said Heberling.

Established in 1931, the Washington Furnace Inn served as a roadhouse and filling station for travelers along the Lincoln Highway in Laughlintown, located about 3.5 miles east of Ligonier at the base of Laurel Mountain. Laid out by Robert Laughlin in 1797, Laughlintown is the oldest town in Ligonier Valley and became a popular rest stop for wagon and stagecoach travelers along the Pittsburgh-Philadelphia Turnpike, before the town of Ligonier was laid out and became the social hub of the valley.

The smelting of pig iron was a leading industry in the Ligonier Valley during the first half of the nineteenth century, even before the coal and coke industries exploded in the region with the advent of the Ligonier Valley Rail Road. Unfortunately the industry waned when the Bessemer process for making steel was invented; the valley's carbonate iron ore was not conducive to making steel using that process.

Laughlintown contained several active iron furnaces, including Washington Furnace, the namesake for the two-story inn. The furnace was built by Johnston, McClurg and Company in 1809, about a mile north on

An early picture of the popular Washington Furnace Inn, located on the westbound lane of the Lincoln Highway (now U.S. Route 30) in Laughlintown, about four miles east of Ligonier. *Courtesy of Brian Butko.*

the bank of what was known as Washington Furnace Run. Washington Furnace operated until about 1826, was sold and rebuilt in 1848 by John Bell and Company and was reportedly still operating as late as 1855. The ruins of that tapered stone blast furnace are still there.

Washington Furnace Inn has changed ownership multiple times in its over eighty-year history. In earlier days, the inn was operated by Pauline Corna Villa Ottino, who also owned two other Ligonier-area restaurants: the Swiss Chalet (formerly Lincoln Lodge) and the Darlington Inn. Leo Pope was a proprietor in the 1940s. Later, Vincent and Annetta Lamonica owned and operated the place for more than two decades.

In the early to mid-1950s, the inn was owned by Rocco ("Roxie") and Cecelia Rado, a Laughlintown couple who relocated to the area from Pittsburgh and bought the business from Max Sherman. Mrs. Rado sold the business in 1957 and moved to Florida after Mr. Rado was tragically murdered at the inn by a patron in June 1955.

Angela Rado, daughter of the former proprietors, remembered that her parents rarely used the upstairs lodgings except sometimes for friends, family and visiting skiers during the winter season.

"Yes, the building was stone," recalled Rado via e-mail correspondence, describing the basic footprint of the inn during the 1950s, which Heberling and Beck have carefully maintained. "Large, with lots of windows, two stories with a full basement. As you came in the front doors you were looking at the bar, it was large, U-shaped…This was a large room with tables for dining and a couple of game machines—shuffle board, bumper pool."

Rado continued describing the inn:

> *To the right of this room was a much larger room that was the main dining room with a large fireplace at the far end, all hardwood floors and lots of windows. The middle was left open for dancing. I was a really spoiled child and I roller skated through the rooms.*
>
> *To the left of the bar was a small room with a TV, phone booth, [seating] booths and a sofa. It was more used by the family but open from the bar room. The public bathrooms were in the room with the bar. There was a door off the bar that entered the kitchen, very large. My mother and aunt were the cooks. Sometimes there were special occasions where a chef would be brought in. There were doors from both the bar and the kitchen that led to the stairs going up to the rooms…also a full attic.*
>
> *Behind the inn on its property were two small stone houses. They were rented at different times. Both were really cool as I remember. There was a large back porch off the kitchen.*

"It was a fun place to spend a lot of time as a child," summarized Rado.

Throughout the mid-twentieth century, Washington Furnace Inn catered to a variety of local patrons and outside visitors traveling on the Lincoln Highway when it replaced the turnpike, welcoming roadside travelers, skiers, snow bunnies and even auto racing enthusiasts from nearby Jennerstown, Pennsylvania. *Latrobe Bulletin* editor Steve Kittey remembered the inn being a popular hangout throughout the 1970s when the parking lot and roadsides were overflowing with cars and the restaurant was standing room only thanks to crowds spilling in after the races at Jennerstown Speedway. The inn was a great place for hungry patrons to grab a bite to eat. Newspaper advertisements from the 1940s tout the restaurant's chicken and steak dinners and its "fine food and liquors."

The establishment has seen ebbs and flows over the years. Greensburg, Pennsylvania resident Rick Thorne, whose family moved to Ligonier in 1972 and has owned the property behind the Washington Furnace Inn ever since, said that the place has "had a long, varied life," riding surges in popularity throughout the years just like any business. Before Heberling and Beck purchased the Washington Furnace Inn, it was operated as an upscale restaurant under the name of "The Furnace" by Adam and Colombe Fruehauf. With a waning customer base, the place eventually closed.

The entrepreneurs had searched for a viable location for their restaurant for a long time before considering the light sandstone building, whose large size and history as a Lincoln Highway landmark won them over.

"We saw a lot of potential," said Heberling. "It was kind of meant to be. We tried for years to buy places around Latrobe and Derry. For some reason it just wasn't meant to be."

The inn's new owners hope that patrons return to Washington Furnace Inn with memories and stories from the inn's heyday, in addition to their appetites. Heberling said that the only history he and Beck inherited with the building was a vintage picture of the inn—now displayed in the bar—and a hotel registry circa 1940–1950s indicating that the six upstairs rooms were rented to guests.

After purchasing the inn, Heberling and Beck restored the building's stone façade to the original 1930s design. The original establishment featured a dining area with kitchen, hardwood floors with available dance area, a bar and six furnished hotel rooms upstairs. The structure of the two-story sandstone building was kept intact, with numerous arched windows and entryways between the bar and dining area. The dining area features custom-made stained pine tables and benches and a large gas hearth that was converted into a wood-burning fireplace.

The heart of the Washington Furnace Inn is the lounge area that has a brand new bar as the centerpiece. Accommodating up to thirty patrons, the substantial oak and pine bar snakes through the lounge area and even incorporates a piece of the former bar that Heberling and Beck decided to keep. The bar also features a tin backdrop, lighted liquor shelves, a shiny twenty-four-beer tap and custom pub tables with pine tabletops and metal legs crafted by Heberling himself.

Heberling said that he, Beck and Robinson did most of the renovations themselves with help from friends. The trio's renovations included sanding and refinishing the original wood floors, installing new tile, painstakingly repainting the textured ceiling and walls, refurbishing the full-service kitchen and installing a brand new bar.

"It definitely needed TLC," said Robinson.

Heberling and Beck are running Washington Furnace Inn "basically the way it's always been run" since its inception in the 1930s by promoting it as a vintage, family-style restaurant and sports lounge, featuring an outdoor summer dining area and occasional live entertainment such as local bands, disc jockeys and karaoke nights. The pair plans to keep the food sizzling, taps flowing and jukebox spinning at the refurbished roadhouse.

"We want it to be a place where everyone is welcome," said Heberling. This vignette was edited from the original articles published in the *Latrobe Bulletin*. ("Historic Washington Furnace Inn plans to reopen," February 1, 2011, and "Historic Ligonier Valley landmark to reopen," August 20–21, 2011.)

Idlewild Park: Where History Is Eternal and Nature Is King

Pennsylvania is renowned for its rich history of amusement parks, a history shared by generations of families from across the state and even the country. A unique attraction that follows this tradition lies quietly nestled amidst a picturesque setting of rolling hills, thick foliage and vibrant flowers that characterize the Ligonier Valley: Idlewild Park—a place steeped in local history, fond memories and natural beauty.

Idlewild's history stretches back to the nineteenth century and can be considered the Ligonier Valley's first recreational attraction and tourism marketing endeavor. Similar to trolley parks that were created to attract passenger business to the trolley lines, Idlewild was proposed as a complementary recreational facility to the Ligonier Valley Rail Road, and the line did bring many visitors to the park along its main line.

Looking to add to the Ligonier Valley Rail Road's already profitable freight business by adding passenger business, Mellon requested permission from William M. Darlington to develop 350 acres of the attorney's property located between the railroad and the north bank of the Loyalhanna Creek into picnic grounds. With the condition that no timber or trees be cut or injured in any way, Darlington granted the request in a letter dated May 1, 1878, giving Mellon "the right and privilege to occupy for picnic purposes or pleasure grounds…my land in Ligonier Township."

Darlington's land, located in the middle of the Laurel Highlands, was the ideal spot for outdoor enthusiasts. According to a 1900 souvenir booklet of Idlewild, "Its scenery is varied and there is none who cannot find something to interest and please them…All of Idlewild in its completeness stands the ideal park; a very garden of nature, unsurpassed and unrivalled." Still today, the scenery lends to Idlewild its distinct and intimate atmosphere, complementing the many attractions within the park.

Floral Scene, Idlewild Park, near Latrobe, Pa.

This vintage postcard depicts a typical floral scene in Idlewild Park. The beautiful flowers and foliage in Idlewild Park enticed city folk to visit Ligonier and spend a day in the country. *Courtesy of Idlewild Park Archives.*

This picture shows patrons enjoying a nice outing in Idlewild during its early days. The lake is skirted by the Ligonier Valley Rail Road, which brought visitors to the park. *Courtesy of the Pennsylvania Room, Ligonier Valley Library.*

This postcard shows the picturesque bridge and lagoon at Idlewild Park. *Courtesy of the Pennsylvania Room, Ligonier Valley Library.*

As an integral part of Idlewild Park's history, the Ligonier Valley Rail Road ran right through the property and helped to promote the park over the years. Its heritage is remembered and celebrated today; the original building, which was considered the smallest full-service railroad depot in the United States during its time, still stands. Although the railroad was forced to close down in 1952 due to the increasing popularity of the automobile and decreasing freight business, Idlewild remained open and continued to attract patrons.

During the early years, the Mellon family expanded and developed Idlewild into a beautiful rustic park visited by many people from the surrounding area that spent their "idle" time enjoying the "wild" landscape. The park's name may have evolved from this concept. The three man-made lakes added in the 1890s—Lake Woodland, Lake St. Clair and Lake Bouquet—provided visitors with boating and fishing. Flower Island, set in the middle of Lake Bouquet, featured gardens full of vibrant flowers while the rustic Woodlands area offered romantic hiking trails. Pavilions constructed around the grounds accommodated picnics and hosted dances and other large social gatherings.

A turning point occurred in 1931 when Idlewild transitioned from a picnic grounds to a full-fledged amusement park. After evaluating the park's current state—lacking rides, utilities and electricity—Richard Mellon,

This early twentieth-century picture shows a more rustic-looking entrance to Idlewild Park, complete with gasoline pumps. *Courtesy of Cy Hosmer.*

Thomas Mellon's son, partnered with Clinton C. Macdonald, a thirty-five-year veteran of the amusement park business, to form the Idlewild Management Company and take control of the park.

Macdonald convinced Mellon to take a "low-key approach" in expanding the park instead of transforming it into a major amusement park, as Mellon originally intended. Macdonald's plans, however, adhered to William Darlington's original stipulation about preserving the natural woodland setting of the park. With each major building project, each individual tree was taken into consideration; oftentimes Macdonald decided to build around an existing tree. In addition, thousands of shrubs, bushes and trees were planted to supplement the park's beauty over the years.

Unlike the majority of other recreational facilities and amusements in the country that closed down after the Great Depression, Idlewild continued to expand throughout the 1930s with more rides, facilities and electricity. Several important additions were made soon after Mellon and Macdonald took control. In 1932, a large swimming pool was built on Flower Island, complete with a sand beach. Although the sand was eventually removed, the pool remains in the current SoakZone area (Idlewild's water park).

Still a highlight of the park today, the modern three-row carousel that replaced the old merry-go-round was built by the Philadelphia Toboggan Company and consists of forty-eight hand-carved horses and two chariots.

Kiddieland, an area designed to entertain small children, was added to Idlewild Park in the 1950s. The smiling clown still greets visitors today. *Courtesy of Idlewild Park Archives.*

The carousel underwent an exhaustive, two-year renovation in 1984. The Rollo Coaster, Idlewild's first roller coaster and one of the oldest rides in the park, was also created by the Philadelphia Toboggan Company in 1938. Built on a hillside, the out-and-back coaster sweeps riders out along the crest of the hill and brings them back through a valley. The coaster was completely constructed out of wood cut from trees harvested on the park's property using a saw mill built next to the site.

The postwar baby boom of the 1950s fostered an increase in kiddie attractions in Idlewild, leading to the creation of Kiddieland, a section of the park specifically designed for small children. In 1956, Story Book Forest, the brainchild of Macdonald and Idlewild performing clown and engineer Arthur Jennings, was created as a separate attraction next to the park.

The pair combined life-sized displays with human characters to introduce children to the famous nursery rhyme and fairy tale characters with which their parents grew up, such as Raggedy Ann and Andy, Humpty Dumpty and the Old Woman in the Shoe with all of her children. Although the original

Added in 1956, Story Book Forest was originally a separate area from Idlewild but was eventually absorbed into the park. The attraction was the brainchild of former owner C.C. Macdonald and clown and engineer Arthur Jennings. *Courtesy of the Pennsylvania Room, Ligonier Valley Library.*

castle entrance has since been removed, the more than forty attractions continue to greet parents and children in the place where, according to the smiling wooden clown, "Childhood is Eternal and Imagination is King."

The Macdonalds, who acquired ownership of the park in 1951, decided to sell Idlewild in 1983 to the Kennywood Park Corporation, which continued preserving Idlewild's traditional character while developing it in new ways. Story Book Forest and Idlewild were combined into one amusement park instead of two separate areas. The water park craze in the 1980s led to the creation of the H2Ohh Zone around the pool, complete with several water slides. In 2002, Idlewild's biggest expansion to date produced SoakZone, a full water park facility, complete with twelve water slides, a large tipping bucket, the Little Squirts play area and, of course, the swimming pool.

Perhaps the most significant addition to the park after Kennywood took control was Mister Rogers' Neighborhood of Make-Believe—a joint endeavor between the park and the late Fred Rogers, who was a Latrobe native and often visited the park when he was a child. Mr. Rogers was

The recognizable red trolley takes visitors young and old through Mister Rogers' Neighborhood of Make Believe at Idlewild Park where they can see all of the beloved neighborhood characters including Henrietta Pussycat, X the Owl and King Friday. *Photo taken by Jennifer Sopko.*

intensely involved with the project, acting as creative consultant, writing the scripts and providing the voices for all of the neighbors, who come alive through animatronics.

After waving goodbye as they leave the station, visitors ride through the neighborhood aboard Trolley, stopping to invite Henrietta Pussycat, X the Owl, Daniel Tiger and other characters to the Hug and Song party hosted by King Friday. The end of the journey reunites visitors with their favorite Mister Rogers' characters at the castle where they join them in a sing-along.

Today, although modernized and expanded far beyond the original perimeters, "this queen of picnic grounds has neither stood still nor gone backward, but has been forever improving and taking on new beauties." As a theme park in every sense of the word, the newly named Idlewild and SoakZone is divided up into seven distinct areas, complete with themed rides and entertainment. Along with Story Book Forest, Mister Rogers' Neighborhood of Make-Believe and SoakZone are: Hootin' Holler, a recreation of a Wild West Town; Jumpin' Jungle, a large play area for children featuring a tree house, net climb and ball pit; Raccoon Lagoon, a new and improved Kiddieland complete with scaled down rides; and Olde Idlewild, the original section of the park containing the traditional amusement rides such as the Ferris wheel, carousel and Rollo Coaster.

Idlewild's appeal is not limited to its historic and rustic surroundings; the family of workers behind the scenes also generates a warm and inviting atmosphere for visiting families to the park. When asked in 2004 about her long-standing career at Idlewild, Rosemary Overly, an art department veteran for over twenty years, fondly recalled "a wonderful team of people" working together to give guests the experience they come to the park to find.

According to Overly, each job, from painting the smallest refreshment stand sign to renovating each intricate part of the carousel, required careful consideration of how patrons would react to it. With each renovation, Idlewild's artisans and craftsmen tried to convey the same thoughts that the original employees had when they first designed and built the sites. "The kids [here] take their job so importantly," she added. Never breaking character as Snow White or as one of the Wild Bunch, Idlewild employees create a real fantasy world for the children. "They truly believe this is real…We can't take that away," said Overly.

Unlike major commercial theme parks around the country, Idlewild's purpose was never to draw large crowds or generate large revenues with record-breaking rides and attractions, but instead to provide visitors with a picturesque and tranquil place where they can spend time with their families. This family-oriented philosophy, combined with the park's natural woodland setting, sets Idlewild apart from other amusement parks. "We work hard ecologically to keep things as natural as possible," assured Mary Lou Rosemeyer, director of public relations for Kennywood Entertainment.

Idlewild and SoakZone are now recognized as the third-oldest operating amusement park in the United States and a rarity as an original train park. After surviving the Depression, a brief closure during World War II and the thrill park craze, Idlewild remains a popular family outing for residents of the Ligonier Valley and beyond and continues to make improvements to the grounds and add new attractions, including a lazy river ride planned to be added to SoakZone for the 2013 season.

The park has also been nationally recognized by *Amusement Park Magazine* as a three-time recipient of the Golden Ticket Award—a top honor designating it as the "Best Children's Park in the World" for three consecutive years: 2010, 2011 and 2012.

"Our park is unique in what it offers to families with young children. Story Book Forest, Mister Rogers' Neighborhood of Make-Believe, Jumpin' Jungle and Raccoon Lagoon Kiddieland are attractions that you would be hard pressed to find in other amusement parks. Those attractions combined with our family-friendly ride and water park mix provide a unique experience for kids of all ages," said Jeff Croushore, Idlewild's sales and public relations manager, in response to the honor.

Rosemeyer attributed Idlewild's continuing public appeal in a rapidly changing society to the fact that the park has remained generally identical in scope to the Macdonalds' vision in the early twentieth century. The generations keep coming, she said, to a rare place that gives both the young and old the opportunity to share experiences. While embracing its past, Idlewild is continuing to move into the future, combining local history, fond memories and natural beauty into one package.

This vignette was edited from the original version published in the *Westmoreland History Magazine*, volume nine, number two. ("Idlewild Park: Where History is Eternal and Nature is King," September 2004.)

"Sunday, Monday, Happy Days":
Teenage Hangouts in and around the Ligonier Valley

In limbo between childhood and adulthood, dependence and independence, teenagers long for a place to which they can belong and where they can find a sense of purpose in the world. To them, their beloved, everyday "hangout" represents a refuge, escape and a world of their own. The teenage hangout represents freedom.

Today, with the advent of modern technology, the distraction of entertainment and an increasingly mobile society, it is hard to remember a time when kids were happy to go to the corner diner and enjoy a Coke with their friends, a time when they were not content to sit at home with their eyes glued to a computer screen, television set or cell phone. The young enjoyed simple social pleasures.

Stroll around the Diamond in Ligonier, walk down Main Street in Latrobe or wander through Derry Township, and no doubt you will encounter people who still remember meeting their first sweetheart at Rustic Inn, starting their first job working the soda fountain at Valley Dairy or dancing with friends to the live sounds of Chuck Berry and Bo Diddley at Harry's Danceland. While some of these beloved places are lost to history, the surviving venues indicate that a simpler way of life is still treasured and remembered as the young and old continue to patronize them year after year.

The Laurel Highlands not only represented the classic way of life for teenagers growing up in small towns, but it also fostered an interesting phenomenon of popular local teenage hangouts that had the power to draw kids from many cities and towns throughout not only Westmoreland County but all of western Pennsylvania. Ligonier was no exception.

According to Ralph Kinney Bennett, former *Reader's Digest* editor and Rector, Pennsylvania native who returned to Ligonier after his retirement, during the golden age of American life after World War II, most small towns and cities throughout the country had their own local soda fountain, ice cream parlor or eatery where kids gathered on a daily basis.

In towns and cities like Ligonier and nearby Latrobe, teenagers would meet at their favorite local hangouts during their lunch breaks, after school or following a show at the local theater. In Ligonier, as soon as the school bell rang, high school kids would sprint over to the Dairy Dell on North Fairfield Street or the Blue & White Dairy Lunch on West Main Street and stuff themselves into the booths, eating burgers and gabbing with their friends. In

This image shows the Lincoln Highway (U.S. Route 30 after a numbered highway system was established in the 1920s) west through town. On the right are the Valley Restaurant and the Blue & White Dairy Lunch. The latter was a popular hangout for Ligonier teenagers. *Courtesy of Brian Butko.*

the evenings, they would return with their dates and drop a few nickels into the jukebox until it was time for their parents to pick them up.

"I can remember myself," mused Bennett, "the first thing on your mind sometimes at the end of the day was you wanted to be at…some place where the kids got together. It was just imperative—that's where you wanted to be, that's where you got away from your parents and everybody else, and that's where you went." Those places were important social centers for teenagers in the Ligonier Valley.

Ice Cream Joe's Valley Dairy

One place that many people remember vividly is Valley Dairy, a local restaurant chain with ice cream parlors sprinkled in several towns along the Lincoln Highway, including Ligonier, Latrobe and Greensburg. The Ligonier branch was located on the southeast corner of the Diamond.

The Gruebel family has been involved in the ice cream business since the late nineteenth century when Joseph A. Gruebel became the first person to commercially manufacture ice cream in Westmoreland County. He churned out the frozen treat in Derry, Pennsylvania, in 1884 and passed along his knowledge and techniques to his grandson and Valley Dairy founder Joseph Fleming Gruebel.

Joseph F. Gruebel opened the first Valley Dairy store in 1938 at 313 Main Street in Latrobe during a time when retail ice cream chains and "dipping counters" were beginning to gain popularity with the public. Naturally, the Gruebels offered their homemade dairy treat at their stores. Mr. Gruebel was fondly known as "Ice Cream Joe," an endearing moniker that has stuck with the business through the years.

By the end of the 1940s, Ice Cream Joe's one little store in Latrobe had multiplied into several throughout through the county, including Ligonier. As his business grew, Mr. Gruebel stopped hand-churning his ice cream far into the night after his restaurants closed and set up the Fairfield Dairy to supply an increasing number of customers with Ice Cream Joe's sundaes, milkshakes and, of course, banana splits, which were invented in 1904 by apprentice pharmacist David Evans Strickler at Tassel Pharmacy in Latrobe.

Although most of the Valley Dairy stores have disappeared from their original locations, the franchise has successfully expanded into other counties throughout western Pennsylvania. In recent years, new branches opened on U.S. Route 30 in Latrobe and also in Cranberry, Pennsylvania.

This image shows the interior of the Valley Dairy restaurant, located on the southeast corner of the Diamond, circa 1950s. "It was a meeting place for a lot of teenagers," according to Valley Dairy owner Joe E. Gruebel. *Courtesy of Paul Fry.*

With a smile and chuckle, Joseph E. Gruebel, Ice Cream Joe's son and current owner of Valley Dairy, remembered how Valley Dairy was a place where people came to simply spend time with each other and enjoy simple treats such as a hamburger, milkshake or pop.

Since there were no fast food chains or shopping malls at the time, explained Gruebel, many teenagers earned extra money working at the Valley Dairy stores, making friends and even kindling romances along the way.

"It was a meeting place for a lot of teenagers," Gruebel recalled. "Before all the franchise people came along…one of the few places to work was Valley Dairy. Especially around Latrobe and Ligonier we would have a number of young people working. And they used to always say we had so many people who went through the 'Valley Dairy Academy' it was almost like a college itself."

Theaters

With television only in its infancy in the late 1950s, kids turned to movie theaters for entertainment—and relief—during the summer, as the theaters were some of the first places to install air conditioning.

Instead of the jumbo thirty-screen theater complexes prevalent today in major shopping areas, small towns and cities had their own local theaters. Some even had multiple theaters clustered in proximity to each other, a trend that points to the massive popularity movies had acquired by the mid-twentieth century. Ligonier had several theaters in the same vicinity, including the Ligonier Theater and the Vox Theatre, both on West Main Street. The Ligonier Theater fortunately continues to operate today as the home of the Valley Players of Ligonier, who host live stage productions. It also continues to show classic movies each weekend.

On Friday nights, many teenagers hoped to steal a kiss from their sweethearts up in the dark balcony of the Gem Theater, on Second Avenue in neighboring Derry Township. Nancy Piper Gibb, daughter of the late owner Fred Gibb, remembers how her father often patrolled the balcony, with its unique entrance located outside the theater itself, shining his flashlight on those "boys and girls [who] smooched a little bit."

Drive-in theaters also became regular hangouts and date night activities for teenagers during the late 1950s and into the 1960s. Although Ligonier did not have a drive-in theater, from spring until fall, many teens lined up their cars at Latrobe's Hi-Way Drive-in on U.S. Route 30 to catch a double feature on the giant outdoor screen, munching on concession stand snacks and snuggling down deep into their seats.

Sadly, many drive-ins theaters have been gobbled up by commercial development. After sixty-four years of hosting movies under the stars, the Hi-Way Drive-in closed following the 2010 season, and its big screen,

The Ligonier Theater, located on West Main Street, continues to show classic films and is now home to the Valley Players of Ligonier. *Courtesy of the Pennsylvania Room, Ligonier Valley Library.*

which loomed high over the four-lane highway, was razed to make way for a pharmacy chain. Instead of a glowing screen breaking up the skyline, a nondescript building sits at the corner of U.S. Route 30 and Theater Street.

Dancing Days in the Valley

For teenagers, the weekend was a time to cut loose and dance. The big band era in the 1940s and 1950s brought a new popularity to, and need for, dance halls and pavilions like the Rustic Inn in Rector, Camp Comfort in Darlington, the Red Rooster near Greensburg and the outdoor band shell at Ligonier Valley Beach. Before and after World War II, these nightspots were packed full with teenagers on weekends and in the summer. In western Pennsylvania, the first wave of the dance craze came with the swell of hillbilly music and square dancing; places like Stahlstown Ridge and Latrobe's Buvett Inn and Beatty Inn hosted square dances on Saturday nights.

One trendy hangout the teens were talking about was Rustic Inn, a popular dance hall nestled in a small wooded clearing off Route 381 "at the Forks" in Rector. Built just prior to World War II, the venue was often crowded with teenagers from all over the region until it disappeared in the early 1960s.

Built out of wood from old barns by retired streetcar conductor Wayne Walker and his son "Red" Walker, the place certainly had a "rustic" look, with knotty pine paneling and timber columns. According to Bennett, who grew up next to the Rustic Inn, teens would enter through the door at the

Rustic Inn, a popular hangout for valley teens, was located a few miles southeast of Ligonier, in Rector, Pennsylvania. *Courtesy of the Pennsylvania Room, Ligonier Valley Library.*

right end of the building, which opened onto a dance floor surrounded by wooden chairs and tables. Wearing his trademark white shirt, bow tie, apron and glasses, Walker would be stationed behind the extensive dairy bar that wrapped around one corner of the room, and his wife would be busy scooping sundaes and banana splits for the kids who lined the stools in front of the bar. The low stage at the far end of the dance floor featured a state-of-the-art jukebox filled with the most popular music.

After the Rustic Inn first opened in the 1940s, Walker hosted square dances on the lower stage where various country-western or "hillbilly" groups came to perform. These were the first instances of live music and were important teenage social events not only in Westmoreland County but also in Fayette and Somerset counties.

Thanks to the explosion of rock and roll in the late 1950s, the big band dances gave way to record hops and live concerts in the 1960s. And the artists who filled these jukeboxes at Rustic Inn, Danceland and the Ligonier Valley Beach's pavilion also filled these places with screaming and dancing teenagers.

Harry's Danceland, located on the corner of Depot and Jefferson Streets in Latrobe, drew major national groups to perform for western Pennsylvania teenagers, including the Hondells, an American surf rock band that had a Top Ten hit with its cover of the Beach Boys' "Little Honda." *Courtesy of the Latrobe Area Historical Society, with permission from Harry Frye.*

The premier hangout was surely Harry's Danceland at 201 Depot Street in Latrobe, owned and operated by Harry Lattanzio, who former house disc jockey and manager Bob Nolan dubbed the "Dick Clark of western Pennsylvania." Before the advent of large-scale concert pavilions and arenas, local venues like Harry's Danceland drew about 90 percent of the popular acts in America. In 1941, Lattanzio converted the top floor of the old Doherty Hardware Store, on the corner of Depot and Jefferson streets, into a roller skating rink—Skateland—and then decided in 1950 to transform "The Rink" into a dance floor featuring record hops and live entertainment for young people.

Every Friday night Danceland featured record hops led by Nolan, who began spinning records for Lattanzio back in 1955 and continued drawing crowds of teenagers to the place for almost twenty years with his two turntables, amplifiers and bullhorn speakers.

As a high school senior in the 1960s, Willie Ulery (née Dunlap) remembered what a typical Friday night was for her and her fellow classmates:

> *Friday night we would attend the football game at the stadium or a basketball game or wrestling match at Latrobe High School. My mother would drive us into town along with other friends who needed a ride. After the school activity we would walk downtown, sometimes getting something to eat...We would then walk, sometimes run, up the four flights of stairs to Harry's Danceland...There we danced and talked through the evening with friends until mom would pick us up at eleven to go home.*

Saturday nights (and Tuesday nights in the summer) were reserved for live entertainment. Kids entered the double doors off Depot Street, sprinted the four flights of wooden stairs up to the top floor of the red brick building and plunked down their twenty-five-cent admission. Hundreds would pack the former roller rink, pressing against the stage, to see Bo Diddley, Chuck Berry, Frankie Avalon, Fabian, Connie Francis, Conway Twitty, the Isley Brothers (featuring a then-unknown guitarist named Jimi Hendrix), the Ike and Tina Turner Review, Bobby Darin, Dion and the Belmonts, Del Shannon, Jan and Dean and the Four Seasons.

According to Nolan, teenagers who grew up during this time were very fortunate because they experienced the birth of rock and roll and had a unique opportunity to see many of the influential artists who created the music in what would be considered rare, intimate settings today.

"I wanted them to have a good wholesome place...to entertain themselves in the evenings...a good place where they could have fun," said Lattanzio, who has loved watching thousands of kids screaming, skating and stomping on the thick wooden floors since the very beginning.

Dozens of the most popular music groups came right from American Bandstand to the stage at Danceland. "We had the hot spot for the longest time," Nolan recalled fondly. Many local artists also "wanted to come and perform because of the exposure, and we used to pack kids in there every Friday and Saturday." Indeed, Danceland fostered the careers of many of Pennsylvania's homegrown artists like the Skyliners, Tommy James and the Shondells, Lou Christie and Bobby Vinton.

On rare occasions Lattanzio brought in guest DJs to spin records and greet the kids, including KDKA's Clark Race, WWSW's Barry Kaye, WQTW's Stan Wall and WAMO's Porky Chedwick. Wall, who began broadcasting in 1956 and hosted many events at the Ligonier Valley Beach, Idlewild Park and the Latrobe Armory, says that record hops were extraordinarily popular in the days of AM radio. Teenagers followed the local DJs around to dances and events throughout Westmoreland County almost as much as they did the musical groups.

"This was the start of the music. This was the start of an era. The dances were the big thing for the kids. It was their big outlet," he explained.

Harry's Danceland continued to evolve with the changing trends in music until Lattanzio closed the doors to the old brick building around 2005 (although it briefly reopened as Club Ice in 2008).

In the Summertime

One teenage hangout that continues to entice not only teenagers but also children and adults to its blue waters in the summertime is the Ligonier Beach, a landmark that graces the side of the old Lincoln Highway about a half mile east of town.

Moving on to a new business venture after stints as a steel worker and a barber, Italian immigrant Cono "Nick" Gallo turned his attention to building a summertime oasis for local residents, vacationers and urban escapees on twelve acres of swampland along the Loyalhanna Creek in Ligonier. He opened the Ligonier Valley Bathing Beach on July 4, 1925, which boasted a 400- by 125-foot, 1.3-million-gallon concrete swimming pool and a man-made beach. At the time it opened, the pool was renowned as the largest swimming pool in Pennsylvania and "one of the finest in this end of the state," as reported by the *Ligonier Echo*.

While the establishment changed its name a few times, from Ligonier Valley Bathing Beach to Ligonier Valley Beach and now to Ligonier Beach, the layout of the establishment has generally remained the same. However, there have been some changes. At one time, Ligonier Beach did in fact feature a small beach. The sandy area curled around one side of the pool until it was eventually replaced with grass. The pool also used to feature a large slide, diving board and Nick Gallo's famed water attraction: a twelve-foot, tilted wooden wheel that both amused and bruised the screaming patrons it flung into the water. The wheel was removed in 1951.

Besides a cool, refreshing dip in the pool, Ligonier Beach has offered dining, dancing and musical entertainment in various forms over the years, most notably during the big band era of the 1940s and '50s. In the summer, Sunday nights were reserved for big band dances in the pavilion. Couples swooned and swayed under a roofed wooded dance floor to live music belted out by several popular crooners of the day. Gallo attracted many traveling

This postcard depicts Ligonier Beach prior to 1950. The back of this postcard reads: "Ligonier Valley Beach located one half mile east of Ligonier, Penna. on the Lincoln Highway is noted for its most beautiful scenic location and affords not only a good place to spend a day but a chance to swim in pure mountain water. In the background can be seen the Laurel Mountain Range of the Allegheny Mountains." *Courtesy of Cordelia Lindsay.*

Before he became the famous entertainer Dean Martin, a young Dino Crocetti entertained patrons under the stars at the Ligonier Beach dance pavilion. *Courtesy of Cy Hosmer.*

big band artists to perform on stage at the band shell, including Perry Como and Tony Bennett.

Gallo's granddaughter Cordelia Lindsay, proprietor of the Ligonier Sweet Shop, remembers radio jingles advertising those dances, beckoning couples to "come dance under the pulsating blue lights."

Lindsay also remembers that Ligonier Beach housed bands in cottages on-site when they entertained at the venue throughout the summer. The most famous of Ligonier Beach's musical guests to stay in those cottages was the legendary Dean Martin before the Steubenville, Ohio native became a star.

A rumor that has been floating around for many years was that young Dino Crocetti actually worked as a towel boy at Ligonier Beach during the summers before changing his name and achieving success as an American pop singer. However, Lindsay debunked the myth and explained that while Dean Martin was the lead singer of a band that performed at Ligonier Beach, probably a territory band, he never worked there in any other capacity than as a performing artist.

With a giant, refreshing swimming pool, a sandy beach and a large, open-air dance pavilion, by the mid-1960s, Ligonier Beach was attracting up to 2,500 people per day. Teenagers flocked to the illuminated wooden dance floor to dance under the stars on Sunday nights in the summer. For a while the big bands played at the beach six nights a week—until rock and roll moved in.

Throughout its almost ninety-year history in the valley, the Ligonier Beach, as it's now called, has remained a popular recreational spot in the region, offering folks access to one of the biggest pools in the country. It's now managed by the Graham family of Ligonier.

Popular Social Centers

The magnetism of places like Rustic Inn and Danceland was so strong that their owners did not need to invest in overly savvy marketing schemes to bring in business—they had the powerful word of mouth. All they needed was good entertainment built on top of a reputation freely proliferated by their teenage market. News moved through the high school gossip chains; everyone knew where they needed to make an appearance that Friday night.

Many families, especially those from the Pittsburgh area, rode the Ligonier Valley Rail Road or the Chestnut Ridge Bus Line up to Westmoreland County and rented cottages for the summer. Teenagers subsequently discovered the hotspots that drew all of the local kids and reported back to their friends once their vacations were over. Soon, kids from all over western Pennsylvania were driving up on the weekends and mingling with those from other high schools.

The dance halls were packed, with barely enough room to shimmy and shake. In Rustic Inn, while three hundred kids were jamming to Mr. Walker's jukebox and feeding coins into the pinball machines, inside Rustic Inn, at least a hundred more would spill out into the parking lot and perch themselves on top of the log benches, eventually wandering the dark country roads back to their cottages, their flashlight beams glowing like lightning bugs. In Latrobe, police officers often stationed themselves at intersections, redirecting traffic for several blocks on the weekends because of the overflowing crowds invading the sidewalks and filling the streets around Danceland.

Another great attraction of these hangouts was the opportunity for local teenagers to interact with kids from other high schools and even students from Saint Vincent College in Latrobe. "It was exciting to meet girls from Derry and Latrobe and all these other places and dance with them and get to know them, even date them. Great friendships came out of that," said Ralph Bennett. In particular, Harry's Danceland and Rustic Inn drew teenagers from a wide geographic area, including many from Ligonier, Latrobe, Greensburg, Blairsville, Mount Pleasant, Connellsville, McKeesport, Munhall, Duquesne and Pittsburgh.

These Westmoreland County hotspots were not merely ways for teenagers to alleviate boredom; they were significant social centers where kids' lives changed in many ways. "You came out there to see and be seen," explained Bennett. "You came out there to show off your car, and sit around and BS and show off for the girls, and vice versa."

These places also played a significant role in the courtship practices of young boys and girls. Many people met their future husbands or wives either at a Victory Dance at Danceland, hanging out at Rustic Inn or scooping cones behind the counter at Valley Dairy. "In many respects [Valley Dairy] probably was a meeting place for a lot of teenagers that eventually ended up marrying," said Joe Gruebel.

According to Gruebel, who met his wife, Virginia, after she started working at Valley Dairy, the best thing about working there as a soda jerk was meeting girls. One of his favorite stories to tell is about Jim and Sylvia Visconti, a couple who used to work at the same Valley Dairy store as teenagers and recently celebrated their fiftieth wedding anniversary.

"I used to always tease them and say, 'You know, it would take the two of you longer to walk in the cooler to pick out tomatoes than anybody else!'" Gruebel laughed. "Well, of course, eventually they got married."

Teenagers also loved to hang out at these places because they were affordable. One dollar guaranteed you, and perhaps your date, a great time. The late Olie Merlin, former mayor of Derry Township, remembered one of his first dates with a girl from the Hillside community. He took her to see a feature at the Gem Theater and treated her to popcorn, pizza and a drink, all for less than one dollar.

Imagine seeing your favorite rock-and-roll group, or teen idol who was plastered all over your bedroom walls, at Danceland for a mere dollar! Afterward you could treat yourself and your date to a sundae, milkshake or other frozen treat at the Valley Dairy or the Blue Ridge Restaurant—all of which stayed open past midnight for the kids—for only a few extra coins.

"This was the classic '50s way of life—un-caricatured like it is on TV. These places don't exist anymore," lamented Bennett.

This piece was edited from the original version published in the *Westmoreland History Magazine*, volume eleven, number three. ("Sunday, Monday, Happy Days: Teenage Hangouts of the 1940s, '50s and '60s," Winter 2007.)

EPILOGUE

The stories in this book mainly touch on people, places and things that stretch back to times long past in the more than 250-year history of the Ligonier Valley. These stories even reach back to the colonial era when a conflict between competing European powers indelibly shaped the course of American history. In modern times, Ligonier's proximity to the town of Shanksville, Pennsylvania, located less than thirty miles away in neighboring Somerset County, ties the valley to a historic and tragic conflict between cultures that also altered this country's development in the twenty-first century. One of the four planes hijacked by al-Qaeda terrorists on September 11, 2001, United Airlines Flight 93, flew over the Ligonier Valley and crashed into a field near Shanksville after passengers wrestled control of the plane and stopped it from reaching its target.

The story below is one vignette of my personal history as it relates to Ligonier. To commemorate the tenth anniversary of the September 11 terrorist attacks on the United States, the *Latrobe Bulletin* editors asked newsroom staff, former reporters and regular contributing writers to each write a story relating their memories from that terrible day. At the time, I was only a few miles down the road from Ligonier, studying English at Saint Vincent College, a Benedictine college in Latrobe, Pennsylvania, where the campus, like the rest of the country, felt the immediate aftershocks of such a catastrophe. The stories were published in the newspaper throughout the week leading up to the anniversary. The following article was my contribution and was published on September 9, 2011.

I will always remember that September 11, 2001, was a Tuesday. I know this because I was preparing for my Introduction to Sociology class, which met on Tuesdays and Thursdays, as Al-Qaeda attacked our country. I was settling into my sophomore year at college and another year of living "on my own" within the dorms and classrooms at Saint Vincent College.

While getting ready for class, I saw an instant message pop up on my computer from my friend Melissa that simply said, "A plane hit the World Trade Center." Admittedly, I dismissed it, being preoccupied about making it to class on time. She said (rather, typed) it so stoically that it didn't register in my mind that something completely unimaginable had just happened. I left for class as usual.

Shortly after our lesson began, one of the faculty history professors, Dr. Susan Sommers, burst into class and announced that one of the World Trade Center towers had fallen. I think she came in again shortly thereafter to tell us about the other planes. Dr. Thad Coreno immediately dismissed class so that we could go back to our dorms and turn on the news.

The girl who sat next to me, Elissa, turned to me and said that her father and grandmother both lived in Shanksville. Together we raced back to my dorm room and turned on the television to watch the news coverage. By then we had realized the enormity of the situation: Flights 11 and 175 had collapsed the World Trade Center towers in New York City, Flight 77 had crashed into the Pentagon in Washington, D.C., and the passengers of Flight 93 had forced the plane down outside of Shanksville, Pennsylvania, earlier that morning.

Elissa tried to call her family from my phone but could not reach them. Eventually she found out that everyone was safe (despite some debris that landed on the roof of their house), but I remember how worried she was and giving her a hug to try and comfort her because I didn't know what else to do.

Elissa and I were not close friends at all. We had lived on the same floor during our freshman year and ended up in the same sociology class. We were acquaintances, but we really didn't socialize together. Although I can remember her face and her blonde hair, I had to reach back in my memory (and the Bearcats Online alumni directory) to try to remember her name. However, we ended up leaning on each other as we watched this horror unfold together ten years ago.

I called my family at some point, probably in a panic, but I don't recall any of our exchanges. My mom says she convinced me to stay at Saint Vincent rather than come home. I remember hearing that my uncle had seen what was likely Flight 93 fly over his house in White Oak as he was standing outside in the fresh air that morning enjoying an early morning cigarette.

I do remember the Saint Vincent community joining together for a special mass in the Basilica held to help students, faculty and the seminary cope with the tragedy and pray for our country.

I still have my notebook from that Introduction to Sociology class. I only filled about a half sheet of paper with notes that day. We had just begun discussing Karl Marx's conflict theory. The first bullet point in my notes reads "the view that society is not always a harmonious unity; there is always conflict." How chilling that a real life conflict between our country and terrorists was unfolding as I took those notes.

Not long after the September 11 attacks, I remember thinking about the movie night that Student Affairs hosted on the field for returning students the prior weekend. While my friends and I were laughing and enjoying scary movies from a blanket spread across the lawn, none of us had any idea how history, our country and our adult lives would change only a few days later.

This vignette was edited from the original version published in the *Latrobe Bulletin* on September 9, 2011.

BIBLIOGRAPHY

The Ligonier Valley: Crossroads of American History

Anderson, Fred, ed. *George Washington Remembers*. Lanham, MD: Rowman & Littlefield Publishers, 2004.

Cassell, Dr. Frank A. "The Forbes Expedition of 1758." *Westmoreland History Magazine* 14, no. 1 (Spring 2009). Greensburg, PA: Westmoreland County Historical Society.

"Fort Ligonier Held the Key to the West." *Ligonier Echo*, October 11, 1962.

Graham, Jeff. Interview with author. Tape recording. Fort Ligonier, July 27, 2012.

James, Alfred Proctor, and Charles Morse Stotz. *Drums in the Forest: Decision at the Forks, Defense in the Wilderness*. Pittsburgh: Historical Society of Western Pennsylvania, 1958.

Ligonier: A Settled Community

Banas, Drew. Telephone interview with author. June 25, 2011.

Brehun, Deborah. "Ligonier Valley Library Celebrates 65 Years." *Ligonier Echo*, April 28, 2011.

"The Busiest Place in Town—A Long Time Ago." Fort Ligonier Days 1999 Official Program, supplement to the *Ligonier Echo*, October 7, 1999.

"Buyers in Newly-Founded Ligonier Faced Deadline for Building Homes." *Ligonier Echo*, October 11, 1935.

Campbell, Patti. Telephone interview with author. June 19, 2011.

"Cannons Are Removed from Public Square." *Ligonier Echo*, October 30, 1942.

"Flowers Now Beautify St. Clair Grove." *Ligonier Echo*, June 17, 2004.

"Grand Opening Held for St. Clair Grove." *Ligonier Echo*, June 28, 2001.

Hudson, Janet. Interview with author. Ligonier Valley Library, Ligonier, PA, May 27, 2011.

Iscrupe, Shirley G. McQuillis. "A Calendar of the Pennsylvania Land Transactions of Arthur St. Clair. 1766–1818." *General Arthur St. Clair 250th Birthday Anniversary Year Commemorative Issue*. Ligonier, PA: Westmoreland Archaeological Institute and Forbes Road Association, 1984.

Iscrupe, William L. "Echoes of the Past: John Ramsey Buried in Ligonier." *Ligonier Echo*, March 23, 1977.

———. "Echoes of the Past: Opening of the Ligonier Opera House." *Ligonier Echo*, October 27, 1976.

Leberman, Robert C. *The Birds of the Ligonier Valley*. Pittsburgh: Carnegie Museum of Natural History, 1976.

"Ligonier Main Street Now Is Completed." *Ligonier Echo*, July 16, 1919.

"Music Pavilion Dedicated." *Ligonier Echo*, October 3, 1894.

"Old Opera House Being Torn Down." *Ligonier Echo*, March 10, 1915.

"Paved Street." *Ligonier Echo*, September 16, 1908.

"Planting Continues at St. Clair Grove." *Ligonier Echo*, June 6, 2002.

Recorder of Deeds Office. "John Ramsey's Original Plot Plan for Ligonier, March 3, 1817." Westmoreland County, PA, 1817.

"St. Clair Grove's Opening Scheduled for Saturday, June 23." *Ligonier Echo*, June 14, 2001.

Van Atta, Robert. *A Bicentennial History of the City of Greensburg*. Greensburg, PA: Robert B. Van Atta, 1999.

West, Vernie. Interview with author. Ligonier, PA. June 18, 2011.

The Iron Horse in the Valley:
Ligonier's Industrial Revolution

"A Brief History of the Mainline of the Ligonier Valley Rail Road." *Ligonier Valley Rail Road Association*. www.lvrra.org/history.

"Coke Making." *Coal and Coke Heritage Center*. http://www.fe.psu.edu/Information/Community/31527.htm

"Controversial Error Leads to LVRR Change in Procedure." *The Liggie* 8, no. 2 (June 2012). Ligonier Valley Rail Road Association.

"Heritage United Methodist Church: More Than a Century of Christian Service." *Heritage United Methodist Church*. http://ligonierheritageumc.org/Docs/history%20of%20heritage%20bill%20downs.pdf.

Iscrupe, William L. and Shirley McQuillis Iscrupe. *Historic Ligonier Valley Calendar 1990*. Ligonier, PA: Ligonier Valley Chamber of Commerce, 1990.

Kline, Benjamin F.G., Jr. *"Stemwinders" in the Laurel Highlands: The Logging Railroads of South-Western Pennsylvania*. Williamsport, PA: Lycoming Printing Company, 1973.

Ligonier Valley Rail Road Association. "The Ligonier Station Impressed All Who Visited." *The Liggie* 5, no. 3 (September 2009).

———. "LVRR Caters to Passenger Traffic." *The Liggie* 8, no. 4 (December 2012).

Messmer, Daniel. "Lessons in Business: The Ligonier Valley Rail Road." *Westmoreland History Magazine* 14, no. 3 (Winter 2009/10).

Myers, James Madison. "The Ligonier Valley Rail Road and Its Communities." Diss., University of Pittsburgh, 1955.

"Nature's Black Diamond." *Coal and Coke Heritage Center*. http://www.fe.psu.edu/Information/Community/31526.htm.

"New and Beautiful Station for Ligonier Valley Railroad." *Ligonier Echo*, August 10, 1910.

Opatka-Metzgar, Kim. ed. "Quarries of Westmoreland County," in *Caves of Westmoreland County, Pennsylvania*. State College, PA: Mid-Appalachian Region and the Loyalhanna Grotto of the National Speleological Society, 1996.

"William Flinn." *Bridges & Tunnels of Allegheny County & Pittsburgh, PA*. http://pghbridges.com/articles/biography/flinn-william.htm.

Military Heroes of the Ligonier Valley

Bennett, Ralph Kinney. "Alvin Carey, Valley War Hero, Died 50 Years Ago." *Ligonier Echo*, August 24, 1994.

Byers, Benjamin Franklin. "PA National Guard Veterans' Card File, 1867–1921." Digital images. *Ancestry.com*. http://www.ancestry.com.

———. "Pennsylvania Veterans Burial Cards, 1977–99." Digital images. *Ancestry.com.* http://www.ancestry.com.

———. "World War I Draft Registration Card, 1917–8." Digital images. *Ancestry.com.* http://www.ancestry.com.

———. "WWI, WWII and Korean War Casualty Listings." *Ancestry.com.* http://www.ancestry.com.

Carey, Alvin P. "AJHS WWII Jewish Servicemen Cards, 1942–7." Digital images. *Ancestry.com.* http://www.ancestry.com.

———. Citation. *Congressional Medal of Honor Society.* http://www.cmohs.org.

———. *Find a Grave.* http://findagrave.com.

———. "Pennsylvania Veterans Burial Cards, 1777–1999." Digital images. *Ancestry.com.* http://www.ancestry.com.

———. "U.S. World War II Army Enlistment Records, 1938–47." Digital images. *Ancestry.com.* http://www.ancestry.com.

Chernault, Tracey. Email correspondence with author. June 30, 2011.

Craig, Kenneth Robert. Report of Separation from the Armed Forces of the United States.

Craig, Duane, and Helen Weller Craig. Interview with author. Ligonier, PA. May 7, 2011.

Department of Military Affairs. Public Affairs Office. Brigadier General Kenneth R. Craig Biography.

Eidemiller, Maryann. "Risking It All: Civil War Veteran Enters Hall of Valor for Heroic Deed." *Tribune-Review,* October 8, 2000.

Ewing, John C. *Congressional Medal of Honor Society.* http://www.cmohs.org.

———. *Find a Grave.* http://www.findagrave.com.

———. *Medal of Honor Certificate.* October 16, 1916.

Foreman, Chris. "Area Vets Inducted into Hall of Valor." *Tribune-Review.* March 5, 2005.

"Funeral of Private William Tosh." *Ligonier Echo,* July 27, 1921.

Hays, Lisa, Carla Baldwin, and Brad Craig. Interview with author. May 16, 2011.

History of the 110th Infantry (10th Pa.) of the 28th Division, U.S.A., 1917–9: A Compilation of Orders, Citations, Maps, Records and Illustrations Relating to the 3rd PA Inf., 10th PA Inf., and 110th U.S. Inf. Greensburg, PA: Association of the 110th Infantry Pennsylvania, 1920.

"Honor Roll to Be Dedicated at Darlington." *Latrobe Bulletin.* September 1, 1943.

Horrell, Rita. Email message to author. June 29, 2012; July 4, 2012.

———. Interview with author. June 28, 2012.

Iscrupe, Shirley McQuillis. Interview with author. July 2, 2011.

Kraus, Michael. Telephone interview with author. July 1, 2011.

Macdonald, Dick. Telephone interview with author. July 11, 2012

"Memorial Services for Benjamin F. Byers." *Ligonier Echo*, August 28, 1918.

Obituary of John C. Ewing. *Ligonier Echo*, May 29, 1918.

Pennsylvania Distinguished Service Medal Citation. March 3, 1989.

"Reported Killed in Action in France." *Ligonier Echo*. September 25, 1918.

Rose, Kurt. Telephone interview with author. July 9, 2012.

Saylor, Richard. Email message to author. July 5, 2011.

Smith, Robert J. "Crescent Pipe Line: Its People and Places." *Tribune-Review*, February 28, 1988.

———. "Pipe Line's Construction Seems Miraculous Today." *Tribune-Review*, February 29, 1988.

Snodgrass, Jim. Telephone interview with author. July 9, 2012.

Sopko, Jennifer. "American Legion Preserved Past, Looks to Future." *Ligonier Echo*, November 10, 2011.

Tosh, John S. "Nephew Seeks Out WWI Site of the Death of Pvt. 'Will' Tosh." *Ligonier Echo*, July 21, 2005.

Tosh, William. "PA National Guard Veterans' Card File, 1867–1921." Digital images. *Ancestry.com*. http://www.ancestry.com.

———. "Pennsylvania Veterans Burial Cards, 1977–99." Digital images. *Ancestry.com*. http://www.ancestry.com.

Voke, Elaine Cramer, and Cliff Cramer Voke. Interview with author. Ligonier Valley High School, Ligonier, PA. November 10, 2011.

"Waging Urban Warfare." *Focus Magazine*, a supplement to the *Tribune-Review*, November 6, 1988.

Wertz, Marjorie. "Seeking Heroism Across History." *Tribune-Review*, July 31, 2005.

Wolff, Jeanette. "Local Civil War Soldier Honored." *Latrobe Bulletin*, October 12, 2000.

Roads and Recreation: Pennsylvania's Mountain Playground

Butko, Brian. E-mail correspondence with author. January 23, 2013.

———. *Pennsylvania Traveler's Guide: The Lincoln Highway*. Mechanicsburg, PA: Stackpole Books, 1996.

———. *Pennsylvania Traveler's Guide: The Lincoln Highway*. 2nd ed. Mechanicsburg, PA: Stackpole Books, 2002.

Cochran, Amanda. "Life's a Beach: Popular Ligonier Pool Marks 80th Year of Operation." *Tribune-Review*, July 17, 2005.

Croushore, Jeffrey S. *Images of America: Idlewild*. Portsmouth, NH: Arcadia Publishing, 2004.

Darlington, William M., to Thos. Mellon, Esq. May 1, 1878. *Idlewild Park Centennial Magazine*. Ligonier, PA: Idlewild Park, 1978.

Futrell, Jim. *Amusement Parks of Pennsylvania*. Mechanicsburg, PA: Stackpole Books, 2002.

———. "The Idlewild Park Story." *NAPHA News* 14, no. 3 (1992): 3–16.

Gesey, Rita. "Rustic Inn Program Today: 'Rustic Blues: Lost Memories of the Rustic Inn and Blue Ridge.'" *Latrobe Bulletin*, April 26, 2006.

Ice Cream Field. Trade Publication. October 1949.

"Idlewild Park." *Laurel Highlands Scene* (May/June 1977).

"Idlewild Park, Mecca for Young and Old." *Westmoreland Traveler* (August 1971): 3.

Idlewild: A Story of a Mountain Park. Pittsburgh, PA: Rawsthorne Printing & Engraving Co., 1900.

Jacques, Charles J., Jr. "More Kennywood Memories." *Amusement Park Journal* (1998).

"Ligonier: The Town and the Valley." *Pamphlet Guides*. Ligonier, PA: Joseph C. Duval, 1964–73.

Ligonier Valley Library. *Restaurants and Eateries of the Ligonier Valley: A Historical Perspective*. Vol. 1–3. Ligonier, PA: Ligonier Valley Library binder of resources for historic photography show, 2006.

Love, Ruth W. "Idlewild Park Rich in History." *Tribune-Review*, January 30, 1983.

Lowry, Patricia. "Greetings From Ligonier Beach." *Pittsburgh Post-Gazette*, August 20, 1995.

Myers, E. Kay, and Gertrude S., pub. "Celebrating 55 Years of Outdoor Movies...Hi-Way Drive-In a Summertime Favorite." *Around Latrobe: A Magazine for Greater Latrobe* (Summer 2006).

——— "The Memories Linger On...Harry's Danceland Was a Latrobe Institution." *Around Latrobe: A Magazine for Greater Latrobe*. Summer 2004.

Peirce, Paul. "Ligonier Family Gives Up Their Days at the Beach." *Tribune-Review*, April 27, 1998.

Rado, Angela. Email correspondence with author. February 3, 2011.

Root, Joanne. "Storybook Forest: 35 Years of Fun." *Tribune-Review*, July 20, 1990.

Stewardson, Michele. "Valley Dairy Closes Hempfield Restaurant." *Tribune-Review*, February 7, 2013.

"Swimming Pool to Be Opened." *Ligonier Echo*, July 1, 1925.

Wissolik, Richard David, Ph.D., general ed. *Ice Cream Joe: The Valley Dairy Story and America's Love Affair with Ice Cream*. Latrobe, PA: Saint Vincent College Center for Northern Appalachian Studies, 2004.

General

Boucher, John N. *Old and New Westmoreland*. Vol. 1–4. New York: American Historical Society, 1918.

Department of the Interior. National Park Service. "Ligonier Historic District." *National Register of Historic Places Registration Form*. July 11, 1994. Via Pennsylvania Cultural Resources Geographic Information System. https://www.dot7.state.pa.us/ce_imagery/phmc_scans/H101488_01H.pdf.

Irwin, William G. *Historical Ligonier Valley. A Souvenir.* Ligonier, PA: William G. Irwin, 1898.

"Official Map of the Lincoln Highway." *Lincoln Highway Association*.

Wylie, Clarence C., and Vernie Stanislaw West. *Two Hundred Years in Ligonier Valley: 1758–1958*. Ligonier, PA: Ligonier Bicentennial Association, 1958.

ABOUT THE AUTHOR

Jennifer Sopko is a self-described freelance writer, local history detective and retro pop culture enthusiast. A Pittsburgh native who grew up in White Oak Borough, her writing projects mainly focus on southwestern Pennsylvania history with goals of enlightening readers about forgotten and obscure regional history and reinterpreting connections between familiar topics.

Jennifer holds a bachelor of arts degree in English from Saint Vincent College in Latrobe, Pennsylvania. Her writing career began in 2003 when she joined the *Latrobe Bulletin* as a stringer, primarily covering local government meetings in the Ligonier Valley area. Since then, she has also contributed articles for the *Westmoreland History Magazine*, a publication of the Westmoreland County Historical Society, written history features for the *Ligonier Echo* and served as the education correspondent for *Tube City Almanac*, a locally owned and independent online journal featuring news and events in McKeesport, Pennsylvania. In addition, Jennifer is an active volunteer for the Ligonier Valley Library's Pennsylvania Room, where she served as guest curator of a historical photo and memorabilia show in 2009 featuring Pennsylvania drive-in theaters

You can follow Jennifer through her website at http://jennifersopko.wordpress.com.